INDUSTRIAL SCENARIO IN INDIA IN THE LIBERALISATION PERIOD

INDUSTRIAL SCENARIO IN INDIA IN THE LIBERALISATION PERIOD

Dr. A. Ayyamperumal

ABHIJEET PUBLICATIONS

DELHI 110094

ABHIJEET PUBLICATIONS
2/46 Tukhmeerpur Extension
Delhi-110 094
Phone: 011-22960492, 65698474
E-mail: abhijeetpublication@gmail.com

INDUSTRIAL SCENARIO IN INDIA IN THE LIBERALISATION PERIOD

First Published 2008

ISBN 978-81-89886-72-1

PRINTED IN INDIA

Published by J.K. Singh for Abhijeet Publications, Delhi-110 094, Lasertypeset by Gaurav Graphics, New Delhi and Printed at Himanshu Printers, Delhi.

DEDICATED TO
MY BELOVED PARENTS

Preface

Industry and Economic Development must go hand in hand with each other. Industries are the modern temples in India. For that purpose alone Pandit Jawahalal Nehru gave much emphasis to the manufacturing and industrial sectors.

In India the Industrial sector has underwent radical changes in recent times.

Nowadays there is an urgent need for the widespread achievement of social development and rural change because of the introduction of New Economic reforms which would unnecessarily created rural urban divide and social inequalities.

In the line of new Economic policy monetary reforms activated tremendous in all fields of Economic development.

This book makes an attempt to analyse and provide a bird's eyeview of the Corporate and Industrial Scenario in post-reform and post-liberalisation India.

I sincerely thank God Almighty for his blessings in completing my Project work successfully.

With immense pleasure, I express my heartful thanks to my guide and Mentor Dr. P.S. Mohan M.A., Ph.D., formerly professor & Head of the Department of Economics National College Trichy-1, for his inspiring guidance, invaluable suggestions constructive discussion and encouragement during this project work.

I am equally thankful to my beloved Wife A. Usha Rani and my Daughter.

I express my sincere thanks to my respected Uncle & Sister Mr.M.Arunachalam & Mrs.A. Malathi Sri Akila & Co. Mailam, Trichy for their endhuastic and financial support to bring out this book in an efficient manner.

I thank Sh. J.K. Singh, Proprietor Abhijeet Publications New Delhi, and Mr. P. Manivannan, MBA and Mr.K. Prabhu and R. Vicky for their timely computerization with great care and effort.

Next I leave it to the Readers,

Suggestions for improvement are welcome.

Dr. A. Ayyamperumal

Tiruchirappalli

Contents

1

Competition in Indian Manufacturing Industries: A Mobility Analysis

One important expected outcome of reforms is an increase in competition and efficiency. While several studies have dealt with the efficiency aspect, there are not many studies on competition. The few studies that have emerged in this area have, however, dealt with the static aspects of competition. While static measures cannot be rejected outright it seems equally important to supplement them with dynamic aspects of competition as well. This is because competition is multidimensional in nature, and for a proper understanding of competition we need to have different kinds of evidence.

In the literature the mobility of firms in an industry is identified as one important dimension—a dynamic one, of what constitutes effective competition. According to Singh and Whittington, the study of mobility of firms in an industry by enquiring in to the amount of mixing and reordering that takes place in the size ranks of individual firms, focuses on dynamic aspects of industrial structure. In this context it would be useful to point out here that public policy might be concerned more with a measure mobility of firms or the turnover of firms in an industry, which will provide the better index of what constitutes "equality of opportunity" rather than the usual measures of concentration. In the discussions on what constitutes effective competition, Ijiri and Simon point out that a "frequent and sizeable change in the ranks of firms in an industry would indicate vigorous competition in an industry. On the other hand if the ranks do not change frequently, it is an indication of little competition." On measuring the dynamic of competition, according to Baldwin, "much of what happens during the competitive process will be manifested by changes in relative firm position. Mobility measures provide a direct measure of the intensity of competition".

Again, the turnover measure can throw light on important dimensions of competition, which cannot be captured by the structural indices such as the concentration ratios. For instance then-firm concentration ratio can remain the same, but the identity of the firms in the group can change because of competition this can be captured only by the turnover measure. Besides, for identifying the market structure of an industry an understanding of the transition of firms is essential. In short given the multidimensional nature of competition and the special attributes of rank analysis, it is an important "structural indicium" for understanding competition.

This, however, does not mean that this measure is free from controversies. One major debate in the literature is the utility of the turnover, index as a measure of market behaviour. At one end you find this measure being encouraged as a useful tool for measuring competition and a replacement of concentration ratios, while at other end where others who did not consider it a useful concept for the reason that it recorded events of little economic significance and dismissed it as a useless measure. Midway between the two some find it a useful supplement and additional indicia for understanding competition. Our critical review of the literature has led to the conclusion that if the limitations of the turnover index are taken care of, it can provide several important insights on competition which cannot be captured by other indicators and is therefore an important tool for analysing competition.

The objective of this paper is therefore to device an improved turnover index, which overcomes the limitations of the traditional turnover index, and to apply it for measuring industrial competition. More specifically, using the new method this study examines the mobility of firms in the India manufacturing sector for the post–reform period.

Towards this end, the specific objectives of this paper are the following: *(1)* critically examine the turnover index and provide an alternative; *(2)* using the new index, test the stability of size ranks and analyse the changes in the degree of mobility; *(3)* study the change in size distributions of industries and their inter-and intra–class mobility; *(4)* test for the relationship between the dynamic index of competition and the direction of mobility of firms among manufacturing industries.

The paper is organsied into four section I gives the data and concepts used. Section II examines the main criticisms against the traditional turnover index and provides an alternative. Section III gives the empirical results based on the new turnover index followed by the summary and conclusions in section IV.

Data Sources and Measurement of Variables

The period of study for the analysis is from 1998-89 to 2000-01 one that largely coincides with the period of reforms. Data related to financial not to calendar years as seen by the over lapping of the year throughout the paper. In order to test this model we require firm level data. The best published source available for this purpose is the data assembled by the Centre for Monitoring Indian Economy (CMIE) in electronic from commonly known as prowess the nature of this data is such that the sample size changes every year, some being added. In other words the database is an unbalanced panel. The reasons for this are probably non-availability of data and need not necessarily imply entry and/or exit of firms in our analysis with this data, forcing us to consider only a balanced panel (firms that have existed throughout the period) covering the period 1988-89/2000-01. By this criterion, we have 14 industrial groups covering a wide range of products as seen from table 1.

Measurement of Size

In the literature various measure of size such as net value added, sales, total assets and employment are used and the problems associated with them are discussed in detail and there is no agreement on the best measure of size variable based on a correlation analysis amongst the there commonly used measure for which we have data.

Table 1: Sample Size of Balanced Panel by Industry Group, 1988-89 to 2000-01

S.No. (Size)	Industry	Sample
1	Beverages and tobacco	14
2	Cotton and blended textiles	51
3	Drug and pharmaceuticals	30
4	Electrical machinery	47
5	Electronics	30
6	Food products	41
7	Iron and steel	25
8	Metal products	22
9	Non-electrical machinery	59
10	Non-ferrous metals	16
11	Non-metallic minerals	48
12	Synthetic textiles	22
13	Transport equipment	72
14	Wood and paper	20
15	All industries	497

Source: CMIE, prowess (1997, 2001).

Correlation coefficients between various measure of size (sales, total net value added) haven been computed for 14 industrial group at the beginning of the period, 1988-89, and at the end of the period 2000-01, and the results are reported are reported in table 2. It is interesting to note that all are highly correctly except for one or two industrial for both the year. Since the correlation coefficient between all three measures are quite high and significant, for almost all the industries, they can be interchangeably used. In our analysis, however, we use total net assets as the measure of size.

The New Turnover Index

Although several limitations of the turnover index have been raised in the literature, we focus our analysis on the two major criticisms, most relevant to the measurement of competition, raised by Hymer and Pashigian (1992). The first relates to the rank ordering by size and the second to the relationship between turnover and market behaviour.

The main drawback of the rank ordering of size is that, it shows only whether the size of a firm is higher or lower than another firm but not how much. This is a serious problem in a rank-shift analysis. Hymer and Pashigian using the example of the shoe-industry from Joskow's paper convincingly argue this point. To quote, "At the top of the industry, a difference of rank is large absolutely and relative; some substantial force is needed to close the gap. But the great bulk (say seven-eights) of the rank different in joskow`s sample are trifling absolutely and relatively, and so are changes in rank... such rank changes signify nothing". In other words, while there is almost no competition, such rank shifts signify otherwise.

The second major criticism is that the changes in market shares which is the really significant phenomenon for understanding the market does not get reflected in the rank analysis. Hymer and pashigian graphically illustrate this by examining the changes in the market shares and ranks of two leading firms, ford and general motors, from the US automobile industry. They show that even when there were large changes in market shares, there were no changes in ranks.

In short, the main argument against the use of

rank correlation to understand competition is that it does not take into account size variations. That is, it is based on rank ordered data derived only from the order of the numbers and not the difference between them. Such ordinal measures provide information regarding greater than or less than status, but not how much greater or less. This problem is overcome by normalizing the data through an order preserving transformation as detailed below.

Let there be in firms in an industry and $S_1...S_n$ represent their sizes in the ascending order of magnitude. To get the order preserving ranks incorporating the size differences, the following transformation is undertaken.

Empirical Results

Having devised a new turnover index, we have undertaken there major exercises to get insight into the firms' dynamics and the nature of competition: *(1)* using rank correlation we test for the stability of size ranks; *(2)* we estimate standard deviation of relative ranks using Ijiri-simon methods, for the end point to understand the change in the degree of competition; and *(3)* following hart and pairs and Singh and Whittington, an analysis of the change in size structure and mobility patterns is attempted using transition matrices.

Stability of Size Ranks

To test for stability ranks, rank correlation is used. If the rank correlation between size of firms at two different points of time is not significantly different from zero then there are frequent and sizeable change in ranks indicating competition among the firms. On the other hand, if the correlatition is significant it implies lack of correlatition coefficient can take any value between the two extremes and 1.the empirical results for the sample of industries are given in table 3.

All the coefficients are significant at the 5 per cent level. More importantly they are greater than or equal to .0.90 for five industries out of 14 suggesting a situation of perfect or close to perfect rigidity. It is interesting to note that that perfect mobility does not prevail in any industry although they exist in varying degrees. The varying degrees of mobility can be characterized as low, medium or high mobility according to the value of the correlation coefficient. For further analysis, industries with a coefficient of less than 0.50 are treated as those with high mobility, between 0.50 and 0.75 as those medium mobility and above 0.75 as those with low mobility. By this classification we have only one industry with high mobility (non-metallic minerals). In the medium category we have seven industries, drug and pharmaceuticals, electronics, food products, metal products, non-ferrous metals, synthetic textiles, and wood and paper. The remaining six industries fall in the category of those with low mobility. They are beverages and tobacco, cotton and blended textiles, electrical machinery, iron and steel, non-electrical machinery and transport equipment. It is worrying to note, that about 43 per cent of the industries are characterized by low mobility and barriers to mobility in varying degrees exist in all the industries considered for the analysis.

However, what is important to our analysis is that one should not only test for stability of ranks and infer from it whether size structure is mobile or rigid, but it should be supplemented with information on the change in the degree of mobility over the Period, that is, the average amount of shifting in the ranks during the period. This would indicate whether competition has increased/decreased in the manufacturing sector.

Ljiri and Simon suggest a measure for this – a measure based on the beginning and the end of the period for such an analysis. This measure is defined as the standard deviation of $q_i = r_i /$ where *r* is the rank of the it firm at the end of a period and *r* is its rank at the beginning of the period. The standard deviation of 'q' is an indicator of the average amount of shifting in rank during the period. We have carried our this exercise, as suggested by ljiri-Simon, for all the 14 industries for the two consecutive years at the beginning, 1988-89 and 1989-90, as well as at the end, 1999-2000 and 2000-01, of the analysis. The results are given in Table 4.

From Table 4, it can be seen that in six out of 14 industries the average shifting has come down, suggesting that competition has declined. Out of the remaining eight industries, for one industry (electrical machinery), the average shifting remained the same while for the other seven industries it has increased. This suggests that only in these seven industries competition has increased. The decline in competition varies from 18 per cent to 60 per cent while the increase ranges from 13 per cent to 304 for cent. Again while average shifting in the initial period ranges from 0.002

to 0.051, in the end period it ranges from. 002 to 0.042 implying a decline in the average rate of shifting (upper value). It is also to be noted that the highest average shifting in the initial year was in the metal products industry (0.051), the lowest was in cotton and blended textiles followed by non-electrical machinery. In the end period, it was again metal products (0.042), but the lowest being beverage and tobacco industry followed by non-electrical machinery.

The following trend in average shifting is worth noting. The largest decline in the average shifting (-60.0 per cent) was in beverages and tobacco. The least decline occurred in the metal products industry (-17.6 per cent). The largest increase in average shifting occurred in the wood and industry while the smallest increase was observed in the food products industry. This suggests that the pace of increase/decrease in competition also varies widely among the industries.

To understand whether competition industries remained competitive or became non-competitive and vice versa, we have calculated rank correlation coefficients between the average shifting at the two end points in Table 4. We get a rank correlation of 0.70 suggesting that the position of industries in relation to competition or non-competition does not seems to have changed very much. Since average shifting for all industries has also remained almost the same (0.0180 and 0.0182), it shows that no substantial change in the structure of competition has occurred during the period.

The rank correlation analysis based on the new turnover index and the average shifting measured by Ijiri-Simon index have provided some indication of the presence of competition in the industries. But this does not provide and indication of the impact of mobility on size structure. In order to get insights into this, we estimate standard measures based on the moments of the frequency distributions of industries such as the coefficient of variation, skewness and kurtosis for the end points for all the industries as reported in Table 5.

The coefficient of variation of size has increased in six industries, substantially in the industries of beverages and tobacco and drug and pharmaceuticals, and decreased in the remaining eight industries notably in non-ferrous metals and wood and paper. Next we examine how strong have been these trends in the concentration as indicated by the skewness of the distribution. The interesting feature of the distributions is that all of them are skewed to the right both in the initial and terminal year as in all the industries, there is a concentration of firms in the smaller size/classes for both periods. The asymmetry has increased only in five industries; beverages and tobacco, drug and pharmaceuticals, metal products, non-metallic minerals and synthetic textiles. In the case of peakedness, as measured by Kurtosis, it has increased in four industries and decreased in the remaining 10. In other words, the majority of the cases, the peakedness has decreased.

The analysis of the moments of the distribution clearly shows that mobility analysis is incomplete unless we examine the nature of size structure in general and inter- and intra-class mobility in particular. This is accomplished by undertaking analysis of transition matrices of all the industries, which alone can capture the nuances of firm mobility. This is illustrated with the transition pattern of firms in one of the industries, the synthetic textiles.

When we proceed to draw the transition matrix of firms, frequency distribution of firms by decilewise size-class is estimated for the end points, i.e., 1988-89 and 2000-01. Each size-class is taken as double the previous size-class in order to have geometric intervals for analytical reasons. This helps to capture not only substantial mobility but also enable sharper and clearer interpretation of size and growth. It may be noted that we have taken 5 per cent as a separate size class (though strictly it does not fall within the decile definition) considering the size distribution of firms in our sample. While this analysis basically follows Hart and Prais, Singh and Whittington, etc., we have improved upon their methodology by taking deciles instead of size-class *per se* in order to ensure comparability across time.

Firstly, the transition matrix (TM) shows whether the size distribution of firms has changed or not during the period as indicated by the frequency of the size class given in the last row and in the last column. For example, only in the case of the first size-class, the frequency remains the same. Secondly, TM provides the number of firms moved upward/downward and /or remained in the same size-class. The diagonal element shows the number of firms without inter-class mobility during the period. The left of the diagonal in any row indicates downward inter-class mobility and the right of it upward inter-class mobility. It may be noted that in the first row only upward mobility is possible since it begins with the diagonal element. Similarly, in the case of the last but one row only downward mobility is possible since it end with the diagonal element. As a result, both upward and downward mobility can be captured only in the rows between the first and the last. For example, all the firms in the size-class (first decile-second row) in 1988-89 have moved out either to the higher or lower size-class by 2000-01. More precisely, three moved to second decile-class, two to fourth decile-class and the remaining two moved down to = 5 class by the end of the period.

Another noteworthy feature of the mobility analysis, is that it clearly shows that the identity of firms in a size-class can change even when frequency remains the same. This is best brought out from the first size-class itself. The number of firms is six in the first size-class at the beginning as well as at the terminal year. But the transition matrix shows that two out of six firms in the year 1989-89 moved out, one to the second decile and another to the fourth decile. Another two firms the second decile-moved into the first size-class leaving the size-class frequency constant. Thus, the six firms in 2000-01 are not the same six in 1989-89. This changing identity can happen in any size-class even when there is no change in the frequency within the size-class. The nature of this problem for the remaining industries will be examined later. IN addition to the identity of firms in the size-class, the mobility analysis has implication for the market structure. It depends on the nature and direction of mobility. If mobility is only in one direction, say upward, then industry is getting more and more concentrated. If is on either direction, upward and downward, the firms move towards an efficient scale according to traditional theory of firms under profit maximization. If the mobility is intra-class but not inter-class and restricted to smaller classes, then it indicates the features of dominant-firm-with-fringe competition (DFFC). The DFFC model can be illustrated using the transition matrix of food products industry given in Table 7.

The mobility of firms is concentrated in the left hand top corner of the matrix and within the first two deciles (10 and 20) of the size distribution. Size-rank test of the industry shows that competition among firms in the smaller classes is high but low in the upper deciles. This is also statistically valid. This is an indication that market structure is of the dominant-firm-with-fringe competition. Of course, the market structure is confirmed only if the price-taking behaviour of the firms, as suggested by Basu [1993], is found valid. This is beyond the scope of the present analysis. Let us extend the analysis to all the industries so that main features of dynamic competition can be captured.

The first feature is the changing nature of the size-structure of industries. It may be noted that the class-interval has been reduced to three instead of the six in the earlier transition matrices due to inadequate number of firms within each size-class. However, here again each decile class is taken as double the previous decile class in order to have geometric intervals, as done in the transition matrices. As stated earlier this help to capture not only substantial mobility but also enables sharper and clearer interpretation of size and growth. The change in the size distribution of firms arising out of the transition process for the end points is shown in Table 8.

.The frequency of all size-classes have changed in four industries (electrical machinery, food products, iron and steel, and wood and paper). It is to be observed that in six industries out of 14, that is for about 43 per cent, there is no change in the number of firms in the large size-class. This does not however rule out the mobility of firms in the largest decile to other deciles and vice versa. That is there can be the identity changes as observed earlier in the case of synthetic textiles. Of the six industries with the same number of firms in the largest size-class(> 80) during the period, in there industries (synthetic textiles, drug and pharmaceuticals and non-metallic minerals) there is change in the identity of firms. In these industries, the conventional concentration ratios (N firm market shares) could remain the same but mobility has occurred. This clearly establishes the superiority of the new turnover index over the market share or N firm concentration ration. It provides important insights on inter- and inter-class mobility which alone can give an accurate picture of the nature of competition in an industry.

The second issue, the most important from the industrial organization theory, is the insight given by mobility analysis on the market structure and size-distribution. Although there is no integration of the two in the traditional literature, which is still an unresolved issues as far as industrial economists are concerned, one model that integrates the two is the dominant-firm-with-fringe competition (DFFC). In such models, the size-structure will be skewed to the right and with high intra-mobility within the small size-classes. One industry that has such market structure is the food products as demonstrated in an earlier paper. It may be noted that under u-shaped average cost curves, competitive market structure should have both upward and downward mobility. Since all such interesting patterns of mobility cannot be put down each industry, we provide a summary of the mobility patterns of all the industries during the period in Table 9.

Table 9 provides estimates on the percentage of firms moving in the upward direction, downward direction and remaining in the same size-class by industries during the period. It may be noted that on an average 54 per cent of the firms remain in the same class, 24 per cent move upward and 21 per cent downward in the manufacturing sector. Further, the highest percentages of firms remaining in the same class is in the non-electrical machinery (86 per cent) with cotton and blended textiles and transport equipment showing the same high levels of immobility (82 per cent). The highest upward mobility has occurred in wood and paper whereas in the case of downward mobility it is in drug and pharmaceuticals. Beverages and tobacco does not show any upward mobility and non-electrical machinery indicates very little downward mobility.

If the competitive pressure were high in an industry then it would have higher mobility in either direction under U- shaped cost-curves in the long run. This implies that the measures of competition and mobility should be positively related among the industries. Three versions of the same hypothesis can be formulated if the average cost curves is not of the conventional type. They are: *(1)* upward mobility alone is positively related to competition; and *(2)* downward mobility is alone positively related to competition; and *(3)* both upward and downward mobility are positively related to competition.

Empirical evidence is reported in Figure 1 (a), and 1 (c) with correlation coefficients. Note that the competition is measured by Ijiri-Simon index for the endpoint (1999-2001) and the mobility of firms for the entire period. Thus results show that only the correlation coefficient between total mobility index (upward +downward) given in Table 9 and competitive index is statistically significant. In other words, more competition prevails in industries with mobility in either direction; otherwise it is not. This proves that as mentioned in the literature, it is the mixing and reordering of firms that constitutes vigorous/effective competition.

The analysis implies that public policy for increasing competition should address ways and means of removing mobility barriers in the manufacturing sector.

Summary and Conclusions

One important expected outcome or reforms is to increase competition and efficiency in the economy. While several studies have dealt with the efficiency aspect, there are not many studies on competition. This study tries to fill the gap. Competition being multidimensional in nature needs to be looked at from different angles. In the literature the mobility of firms is identified as one important dimension- a dynamic one, of what constitutes effective competition. At the same time it is also not without criticism. The main criticism against the turnover index (the rank ordering of size) is that it only shows whether the size of a firm is higher or lower than another firm but not by how much. Therefore, the stability of the ranks may not capture the extent of competition. The second criticism is that the changes in market shares which is the really significant phenomenon for understanding the market does not get reflected in the rank analysis.

The contention of this paper is that if the limitations of the turnover index are taken care of, it can provide several important insights on competition, which cannot be captured by other indicators, like the concentration ratio and is therefore an important tool for public policy.

In this paper, we provide an alternate turnover index, which overcomes the limitations of the traditional index through an order preserving transformation of the data provided by CMIE (Prowess) on 14 major industries for the period, 1998-89/2000-01. The new index is tested for rank shifts of 14 industries. The stability between the ranks of the industries for the end points indicates that 43 per cent of the industries have very low mobility. The change in competition examined through ijiri-Simon index indicating average shifting among firms belonging to 14 industrial groups, show that 50 per cent of the industries have shown an increasing trend. But the rank correlation of change in competition or average shifting among the industries over the period does not show any shift in their relative positions during the period. This implies that some rigidity exists in the expansion of competitive forces in the manufacturing sector.

The changing nature of the size structure is examined by the skewness and kurtosis of the distributions. The frequencies of all size-classes have changed in four industries (food product, iron and steel, electrical machinery and wood and paper). It is observed that in six industries out of 14, about 50 per cent, there is no change in the number of firms in the large size-classes. This does not however rule out the mobility of firms from the largest to other smaller classes and vice versa. In other words, the identity of firms in a class can change even when the frequency does not change. Of the six industries with same number of firms in the largest size-class (>80) during the period, three of them (drug and pharmaceuticals, non-metallic minerals and synthetic textiles) exhibit the change in the identities. In these industries, it may be noted, the concentration ratios could remain the same and yet mobility could occur indicating competition.

The inter- and inter-class mobility of firms are examined for its implication for market structure using transition matrices. The analysis gives the following conclusion. On an averages, 54 per cent of the firms remain in the same class, 24 per cent move upward and 21 per cent downward in the manufacturing sector. Further, the highest percentage of firms remaining in the same class is in the non-electrical machinery (86 per cent) with cotton and blended textiles and transport equipment showing the same high levels of immobility (82 per cent). The highest upward mobility has occurred in wood and paper whereas in the case of downward mobility it is in drug and pharmaceuticals. Beverages and tobacco does not show any upward mobility and non-electrical machinery indicates very little downward mobility. The study also links up patterns of mobility with market structure. It illustrates the existence of varied types of competition in terms of inter-and intra-class mobility, which cannot be captured by the traditional concentration ratios. It shows that competition is not associated with either upward and downward mobility.

This study clearly establishes that the mixing and reordering, upward and downward mobility, of firms in an industry, is an important dimension. Any public policy on increasing competition in the manufacturing should give top priority in understanding mobility barriers and suggest ways of eliminating such barriers.

2

Executive Competition, Firm Performance and Governance: An Empirical Analysis

Introduction

Conventional economic theory views the problem of managerial compensation and incentives from a "principal-agent" framework. The division between ownership and management in modern corporations implies that the owners of the corporation (the shareholders) do not control its resources. Corporate control, which is understood as the power to control and use the firm's resources, if widely acknowledged as being in the hands of the organization's managers. Consequently, the standard problem related to the misalignment of owner's and manger's goals has to be overcome to achieve an efficient, wealth (utility) maximizing solution.

Both organizational and finance theories state that the distribution of power among corporate mangers and shareholders has significant implications for firms performance. The problems of managerial motivation, behaviour and compensation can be seen under this larger framework wherein the contractual relationship that is defined to solve these problems ultimately has an impact on how power is distributed between the two groups. The critical questions that arise from this for the shareholders are whom to appoint as managers and how to incentivise them so that their performance leads to wealth maximization after accounting for the costs of such processes. The presence of reasonably well functioning labour markets for managers, consisting of people with the skills to carry out the expected activities, solves the former problem. But historically, it is the latter problem, that of incentivising appropriate behaviour and rewarding performance that has proved to be the more troublesome.

Standard economic solutions for incentives include designing remuneration packages that are "tied" to either firm performance or increases in shareholder wealth. This is usually achieved by a number of ways including performance-based variable pay or commission, stock options etc. However, such measures in isolation do not solve the problem of alignment of objectives. The question of how such a solution is arrived at and the role played by each party in such a process still remains. Economic theory states that the right to appoint gents and fix their compensation (a "control" right under the principal agent frame work) Should always be in the hands of the principals, i.e., the shareholders (as opposed to the "decision" rights that are needed to run the corporation, which can be delegated to the agents). However, given that most shareholders in a corporation are dispersed and do not own a "controlling" stake in the firm, it often becomes too costly to be involved in this process. In effect, the agency costs increase. This has severe implication for the problems relating to fixing managerial compensation, i e, are the shareholders, in effect, giving up their control rights when they do not actively participate in the decision-making process?

The functioning of a board of directors in modern corporations serves as a mechanism for institutionalizing the process of fixing managerial compensation and monitoring performance, thereby ensuring that the wealth maximization objective of the shareholders is maintained. The members of the board have the responsibility of ensuring that the interests of the shareholders are upheld and that the actions of the managers do not sideline them in any way. In effect this mechanism places certain restraints on the power that managers enjoy and the degree of control that they can exercise on shareholder wealth.

At the same time, members of the top management like the chief executive officer (CEO) are often members of the board. So there is a possibility of collusion between the members of the board leading to a situation where in the process of "incentivising" performance in the interests of the shareholders may break down. It is here that factors like board composition and division of responsibilities among board members become important.

In recent years, the notion of "corporate governance" has gained a lot of attention in the study of corporate objectives and performance. Corporate governance is commonly understood as the set of processes and conventions that affect the way a corporation is directed, administered or controlled. The principles of corporate governance lay out a set of practices that the board of directors needs to adopt to ensure economic efficiency and the alignment of interests between all the stakeholders of the organization. In the context of executive compensation, good corporate governance requires certain mechanisms in the process of fixing compensation and monitoring top management performance. These include the presence of "independent" directors on the board, division of responsibilities between the chairman and the CEO and the establishment of compensation committees. The strengthening of corporate governance norms all over the world and the increasing importance given to it by financial markets has forced companies to adopt suitable reforms in their compensation policies for top executives.

In the Indian context, the issue of executive compensation has been seen with greater interest since the start of economic liberalization in the early 1990's. The post-liberalisaion period has also seen a steady increase in managerial salaries at all levels. Increasing profitability of companies, competition in the market for managerial talent and the practice of benchmarking company policies with global standards have all contributed towards the rise in executive compensation. All these changes have resulted in new ways in which top management compensation is decided and enforced in Indian companies. Another feature unique to the Indian context (vis-à-vis western countries) is the dominance of "family-owned" companies. These companies in effect have "owner-managers", with the same group of people who own the company being members of its top management. Therefore, the study of compensation policies in the Indian context can potentially serve as a useful way of analyzing the effect of the presence of owner managers.

This paper attempts to establish the interrelationships between executive compensation, firm performance and various corporate governance parameters by studying a large sample of Indian companies. A linear regression model that captures compensation data along with key financial performance and corporate governance parameters is used to explain the determinants of executive compensation.

The rest of this paper is organized as followed: Section II contains an overview of the existing literature on executive compensation, firm performance and other factors. Section III describes the empirical model used and hypotheses tested. Section IV describes the data that has been used for this study. Section V presents and discusses the results and Section VI provides a conclusion and suggests possible future research themes in this area.

Literature Review

The link between executive compensation and corporate performance has been explored extensively in western countries, especially in the US. Public debate in these countries revolving around executive compensation focuses mainly on the link between company performance and executive compensation reflects company performance is a controversial one, with different authors taking up widely different positions on the issue.

Murphy (1986) states that the belief that top

executives in companies are excessively paid is flawed and displays a lack of understanding about the managerial labour market. He points out that cross sectional studies that analyse executive compensation across companies at a point in time cannot point out the correlation between pay and performance over time for a company that can provide insights into whether pay and performance are correlated. Such a study showed that pay and performance of top executives are strongly and positively correlated. Besides this, short-term and long-term incentive plans benefit shareholders by "incentivising" mangers to perform better in their interests.

In a similar vein, Jensen and Murphy (1990a) question the importance of excessive compensation in public debates. They instead propose that it is the mode in which CEOs are paid (cash, stock options, bonuses, etc) that should be analysed rather than just focusing on how much CEOs are paid. Based on a large sample of data on executive compensation spanning half a century, they conclude that changes in compensation do not reflect changes in corporate performance because a $ 1,000 change in market value of a company resulted in just 6.7 cents increase in the salary and bonus of the CEO. They go on to recommend that in the shareholder's interests, managers need to be given big rewards for outstanding performance and suitable penalties for underperformance.

Murphy and Jensen (1990b) also state that the level of pay affects the quality; of managers an organization can attract. They argue that if pay and performance are not strongly correlated in companies, the phenomenon of "corporate brain drain" where the most skilled persons will self select into other rewarding professions (like lawyers, consultants, etc.) is inevitable.

Another interesting area of research regarding executive compensation is whether the level and mode of compensation has any effect on future firm performance. Abode (1990) using a data set of more than 16,000 managers in 250 large corporations in the early 1980's shows that paying an incremental 10 per cent bonus for good performance results in a 0.3-0.9 per cent increase in economic performance in the subsequent fiscal year. Further, paying an incremental 10 per cent bonus for good stock performance results in a 4 per cent–12 per cent increase in stock performance in the subsequent period.

The board them in the above studies is to study is to study the relationships between pay and performance and the effect of modes of compensation like stock options, bonuses, etc. The underlying assumption is that structuring suitable compensation contracts can serve as a remedy to the principal agent problem.

There have been attempts to develop alternative explanations for executive compensation different from the above approach. One of the alternative frameworks is that of "managerial power". According to this approach, the design of executive compensation contracts is seen not as a part of the principal agent problem, but as a part of the principal agent problem itself. According to Bebchuk and fried (2003), managers are in a position to affect their own pay and will do so in a way that will weaken the link between their pay and performance. They question the effectiveness of the board of directors to fix an effective compensation contract and monitor managerial performance. Since the executive director on the board (consisting of the

CEO and other top managers) wield influence on the appointment and compensation of the other members of the board, there is the possibility of collusion as the other directors can maximize their utility by either seeking reappointment or increasing their remuneration with the help of the CEO. Consequently, there is little possibility of arms length bargaining between the board and the top management when deciding the compensation contract.

The increasing importance given to corporate governance in public discussion about corporate performance has led researchers to study the impact of various corporate governance parameters on executive compensation. The focus of such studies has been to explain the differences in compensation across firms based on the differences in corporate governance practices.

Pukthuanthong et al (2004) and Talmor and Wallace (2001) studied CEO compensation in the US financial services sector. They found that corporate governance parameters like board characteristics and ownership structure are leading determinants of pay variation across firms. Davila and Penalva (2004) find that weak corporate governance results in compensation contracts that put more weight on accounting measures rather than market based returns. They also report that weaker corporate governance is associated with lower variability in executive pay and higher cash components of total pay.

The above results are corroborated by Core et al (1999) by studying a sample of large US firms over a three-year period. They report that variation in CEO compensation across firms is explained to a significant extent by board and ownership structure. CEOs also earn greater compensation when corporate governance structures are less effective. The conclusion being that firms with weaker corporate governance mechanisms face higher agency costs and the CEOs of such firms earn higher levels of compensation.

It must be noted that the way corporations are governed varies significantly across countries due to the differences in institutional and legal frameworks. Countries in North America and western Europe have well evolved systems of corporate governance unlike countries in eastern Europe and Asia where the introduction of western style corporate governance practices is a recent phenomenon. At the same time, most of the studies on executive compensation have been carried out in the context of American and European organizations. Management authors like Khhanna and Palepu (1997) have pointed out the significant differences in the "institutional context" in which firms in emerging markets operative. The institutional contexts is defined as the set of product, capital and labour markets along with their associated regulatory and legal systems. The authors argue that the capital and labour markets are quite underdeveloped in these countries. In light of this, the relevance of research on executive compensation carried out in western countries in the context of emerging economies can be questioned.

The work by Fung et al (2001) is an attempt to examine the issue of executive compensation on the Chinese context. They find that corporate governance has a significant impact on compensation. However, the nature of relationship between variables is quite different from earlier studies. Firms with a larger number of directors tend to restrict CEO compensation which is in contrast of studies carried out in the US.

In the Indian context, interest in the study of managerial labour market and executive compensation has increased only in the last 10-15 years. The effect of economic liberalisation along with the wide-ranging changes in the market for managerial talent has resulted in significant changes in the compensation policies adopted by Indian companies. The issue has also seen greater public attention (especially seen in the business press in India) even though there have been very few debates on the excesses of executive compensation. Annual compensation surveys are now a common feature in business magazines and newspapers. In one such recent survey, Swami (2005) reported that CEOs of many Indian companies saw salary increases of the order of 300 per cent in the year 2004. The study also reported that variable pay is increasingly becoming the highest contributor to the salary package.

There have been very few empirical studies on the determinants of managerial compensation in the Indian context. Bhattacherjee et al (1998) explored the effects of economic liberalisation on managerial compensation policies in Indian firms. They hypothesized that the pay of executives became more sensitive to firm performance after liberalisation. Using 237 CEO years of data covering the period before and after liberalisation, it was found that an Rs 100 increase in either sales or shareholder's wealth increased the pay of the CEO by 15 and 22 paise respectively. Accounting based performance measures were not found to be significant in explaining CEO pay. There was also a clear increase in sensitivity of pay to firm performance post liberalisation in large firms.

Ramaswamy et al (2000), using a sample of the top 150 Indian firms hypothesized that human capital, firm performance and corporate governance variables jointly determine CEO remuneration. They found that firm size was not a significant explanatory variable of CEO compensation, rather firm performance (as measured by Return on Assets) was. Family ownership of a firm was negatively related to CEO pay. The authors explain this by postulating that family ownership and management significantly reduces the divergence of interests between managers and sharefolders. They also found that CEO duality (I e, the same individual occupying the CEO and chairman positions) and the proportion of insider directors has no relation to executive compensation in family owned firms whereas they are key variables in explaining compensation in non-family owned firms.

Ghosh (2003) studied the compensation of the board of directors along with CEO compensation to capture the effects of inefficient monitoring by the board. The model that was used included firm performance, corporate governance and corporate diversification measures as determinants of CEO and board compensation. Using data from a large number of firms in the manufacturing sector, it was found that board compensation depends on current and past year performance while CEO compensation depends on only current year performance. Conventional personal attributes of the CEO like education, experience etc, were found to be ineffective in explaining CEO compensation. Firm size was found to be a significant variable in explaining inter-firm differences in compensation.

This paper attempts to integrate the approaches followed in the above works by looking at multiple factors including firm performance, sharefolder wealth changes and corporate governance parameters to develop an explanatory model for executive compensation in Indian firms. The data set used is recent and large, covering a wide cross section of firms across industries. This paper considerably adds to the Bhattacherjee et al (1998), Ramaswamy et al (2000) and Ghosh (2003) papers while incorporating features from all of them.

Empirical Procedures

This paper deals with four broad sets of factors that jointly determine executive compensation in Indian firms: firm performance, firm-specific characteristics, sharefolder wealth changes and key corporate governance parameters. Thus, our basic model is:

Executive Compensation = f (firm performance, firm characteristics, sharefolder wealth, corporate governance indicators)

Two different aspects of executive compensation are modelled in this paper. They are total pay of the CEO and the ratio of variable (or incentive) pay to total pay of the CEO. It is assumed that the same set of independent variables determine both these dependent variables.

Executive Compensation and Firm Performance

There are a number of ways to measure firm performance, but the easiest and most commonly used method is to use its financial performance measures. Definitions of financial performance measures are quite standardized and used widely to study firm performance. It is also easy to obtain as public limited companies have to publicly disclose their financial results to fulfil regulatory requirements.

Out of the number of financial performance measures available, profitability measures are used in this study to measure firm performance. These profitability measures can be derived from the accounting information that firms disclosed periodically. Two of the most commonly used profitability measures are net profit margin (NPM) and return on assets (ROA). Being ratios, these measures are normalized for any size effects among different firms.

The use of incentive or performance-linked pay, as a tool to motivate managers and induce risk taking, has been widely recognized in their economic literature. An employment contract that contains provisions for incentive pay will result in managers being paid higher amounts of variable pay on achieving higher levels of profitability. Paying incentive pay in the current period can also be seen as a tool for motivating managers to achieve superior performance in subsequent periods. Therefore, the two propositions above give rise to the first set of hypotheses tested in this paper.

Hypothesis 1A: Ceteris paribus, NPM (or ROA) of a firm and total CEO pay will be positively associated.

Hypothesis 1B: Ceteris paribus, NPM (or ROA) and the ratio of variable to total CEO pay will be positively associated.

The values of NPM and ROA capture the firm's performance in a single time period only. It must be kept in mind that generally the appointment of mangers by shareholders is for more than a single time period. So, shareholders expect managers to deliver profits for an extended period of time. An efficient contract would therefore be one where managers are rewarded for achieving incremental profits across time periods. The effect on compensation can be studied by looking at the values of 'incremental" NPM and ROA where incremental NPM (and ROA) is defined as:

Incremental NPM = NPM − NPM

Where the two values of NPM are for two consecutive time periods (t and t-1).

Using similar arguments as before, it can be hypothesized that:

Hypothesis 2A: Ceteris paribus, Incremental NPM (or ROA) and total CEO pay will be positively associated.

Hypothesis 2B: Ceteris paribus, Incremental NPM (or ROA) and the ratio of variable to total CEO pay will be positively associated.

Executive Compensation and Firm Characteristics

A number of firm specific characteristics can be thought as influencing executive compensation. Earlier studies in the Indian context [Ramaswamy et al 2000; Ghosh

203] have used different characteristics like size, extent of diversifications, complexity of the firm's bushiness and characteristics of the industry the firm operates in. The firm-specific characteristics that are used in this study are:

Firm Size

A number of earlier studies [Core et al 1999; Murphy 1999; Ramaswany et al 2000; Talmore and Wallace 2001; Fung et al 2001; Ghosh 2003] on executive compensation have incorporated firm size as an explanatory variable. The basic intuition behind this is that larger firms will be in a position to pay their managers more because the size of their businesses is bigger resulting in greater revenues and profits (after adjusting for the sizes of their managerial workforces). Some of the studies [Core al 1999; Talmor and Wallace 2001; Ghosh 2003] have also found firms size to be a statistically significant variable in determining managerial compensation. In this paper, firms size is used as a control variable so that any differences in compensation due to firm size across companies in the data set are captured.

There can be a number of variables that measure firm size: revenues, profits, number of employees, etc. In the above studies the sales or revenue of a company from its operations is used to represent firm size. We too use the firm's sales or revenues from its operations as a control variable.

Hypothesis 3A: Ceteris paribus, the sales (or revenue) of a firm and total CEO pay will be positively associated.

Hypothesis 3B: Ceteris paribus, the sales (or revenue)

of a firm and the ratio of variable to total CEO pay will be positively associated.

Firm Being a Public Sector Undertaking

The case of public sector undertaking (PSU) is unique to the Indian context where these companies are owned and managed by the government. From the viewpoint of managerial compensation, there are a few factors that make these set of firms unique. Firstly, the process adopted for deciding managerial compensation in these firms in widely different from the practices in the private sector. Compensation in PSUs is decided by the government and is subject to government rules and regulations, i.e., a "pay commission" model of "administered pricing". The firm on its own has little or no autonomy in deciding its managerial salaries. It has also been reported that the absolute levels of compensation at all levels in PSU s is far less than in the private corporate sector and that the PSUs do not usually adopt any significant incentive pay plans to reward performance [Swami 2005]. Therefore, a dummy variable representing whether a firm is a PSU or not will be used as a control variable in our model.

Hypothesis 4A: Ceteris paribus, total CEO pay will be lower for firms that are PSUs.

Hypothesis 4B: Ceteris paribus, the ratio of variable to total CEO pay will be lower in firms that are PSUs compared to firms that are not.

Firm Being Part of a Multinational Corporation

This study also aims to account for the presence of multinational corporations (MNCs) in the Indian corporate sector. These firms usually adopt policies that closely resemble the compensation policies adopted by them in other parts of the world. This would result in a difference from other Indian firms in terms of compensation policies. Again therefore we use a dummy variable representing whether a firm is a MNC or not in the model.

Hypothesis 5A: Ceteris paribus, total CEO pay will be higher in an MNC when compared to other firms.

Hypothesis 5B: Ceteris paribus, the ratio of variable to total CEO pay will be higher in a MNC.

Executive Compensation and Shareholder Wealth

Since the issue of executive of executive compensation is most often discussed from the perspective of the shareholders it is always instructive to study whether managerial performance results in increasing shareholder wealth buy increasing the return on the investments they have made in the firm. The gains to the shareholders are commonly measured through the appreciation in the value of the stock that they hold. Apart from this, dividends declared by the firm are also a source of monetary gain for the shareholders. The sums of the gains from stock price appreciation along with those from dividends constitute the total returns on shareholders (TRS).

Hypothesis 6A: Ceteris paribus, total CEO pay and TRS are positively associated.

Hypothesis 6B: Ceteris paribus, the ratio of variable to total CEO pay and TRS are positively associated.

Executive Compensation and Corporate Governance

The practices related to corporate governance that a firm adopts can significantly affect the nature of managerial salaries. These practices aim to curb managerial poor in ways that harm shareholder interest while at the same time encouraging behaviour that results in greater economic efficiency. The extent to which good corporate governance practices are followed in a firm can be studied and quantified by looking at a number of parameters. In this paper, four parameters are used; separation of power between CEO and chairman, presence of owner-managers, constitution of the board in terms of independent directors and the extent of institutional shareholding in the company.

Separation of Power between Chairman and CEO

The separation of power between the chairman of the board of directors and the CEO is a key issue in corporate governance. According to Bhattacharya and Rao (2005), a dual leadership structure refers to a situation where the CEO of the firm is also the chairman of the board of directors. A separate leadership structure on the other hand, will have two different individuals occupying the two positions.

Finkelstein and D'Aveni (1994) argued that a separate leadership structure will lead to a greater degree of independence to the board in various issues related to monitoring managerial performance. It is expected that a board that has an independent chairman will be more effective in designing a compensation contract and monitor the performance of the managers in a way that serves the interests of the shareholders.

Hypothesis 7A: Ceteris paribus, a dual leadership structure will lead to higher total CEO pay.

Hypothesis 7B: Ceteris paribus, a dual leadership structure will lead to a higher ratio of variable to total CEO pay.

Presence of Owner-Managers on the Board

The Indian corporate sector is dominated by "family-owned" businesses where either a majority or a controlling stake in the shareholding of a firm is owned by a particular family. The members of the family are also usually part of the management thereby resulting in the presence of owner-managers (very often referred to as "promoters" in the Indian context) at the highest levels of the firm's management. This gives rise to a situation wherein a group of the principals of the firm are also its agents. In such a situation, the principal agent framework cannot be strictly used for analysis as the conventional framework assumes a complete separation between ownership and management.

Ghosh (2003) reported that a dual leadership structure leads to a statistically significant increase in CEO compensation to the extent of 7.3 per cent. On the other hand, Ramaswamy et al (2000) showed that family ownership was not a significant determinant of CEO pay. This presence of owner-managers can be investigated by positing the following hypothesis:

Hypothesis 8A: Ceteris paribus, a CEO who is an owner (or promoter) will receive higher total pay when compared to a CEO who is not.

Hypothesis 8B: Ceteris paribus, a CEO who is an owner (or promoter) will receive a higher proportion of variable to total pay when compared to a CEO who is not.

Independent Directors on the Board

All companies are required by law to appoint "independent" directors on their boards. Clause 49 of the Listing Agreement of the Securities and Exchange Board of India (SEBI) lays down the definition of an independent director. The objective is to ensure the presence of truly independent directors on the board so that they can play an active role in upholding shareholder interests. Regulators have also focused on the composition of the board in terms of the strength of the independent directors. According to the latest amendment to clause 49 of the Listing Agreement of SEBI, the number of independent directors on the board should not be less than half the total strength of the board when the chairman is an executive director and should not be less than one-third the total strength of the board when the chairman is a non-executive director.

With respect to executive compensation, Clause 49 of the SEBI act states that all companies have to constitute a remuneration committee consisting of directors, all of whom are non-executive, with the chairman of the committee being an independent director. It is the remuneration committee that recommends the compensation that is paid out to the CEO and other executive directors on the board. So in theory, the independent directors play a critical role in designing the compensation of the CEO apart from their monitoring roles.

Hypothesis 9A: Ceteris paribus, the proportion of independent directors and total CEO pay will be negatively associated.

Hypothesis 9B: Ceteris paribus, the proportion of independent directors and ratio CEO pay will be negatively associated.

Impact of Institutional Shareholding

Institutional shareholders are institutions that hold substantial blocks of a company's shares and thereby control a considerable number of voting rights to influence board decisions. Typical institutional investors include banks, financial institutions, pension funds, mutual funds, etc. They are different from individual shareholders as it is much easier and less expensive for them to play an active role in shareholder meetings, voice their opinion and ensure that managers need to win their support on matters that require shareholder approval.

Institutional shareholders can play a monitoring role similar to that of the independent directors. They can easily oppose compensation plans for the CEO and other executive directors if they view it as being inimical to their well being as shareholders. Thus, we hypothesis that:

Hypothesis 10A: Ceteris paribus, the proportion of institutional shareholding and total CEO pay are negatively associated.

Hypothesis 10B: Ceteris paribus, the proportion of institutional shareholding and ratio of variable to total CEO pay are negatively associated.

The variables that are used in our model (s), their definitions and predicted relationships are summarized in Table 1.

The Regression Models

Having stated the factors that are proposed to be used as explanatory variables for executive compensation and the associated hypotheses that are to be tested, a standard OLS regression model is used to carry out a cross sectional study of executive compensation. The regression model for total CEO compensation can be written out as:

In (CEO Compensation)=a+b1 (NPM) + b2 (ROA)+b3

(Inc. NPM)+b4 (Inc, ROA)+b5 (TRS)+b6 (CEO-Chairman)

+b2 (CEO-Promoter)+b8 (per cent Independent Directors)+b9

(Per cent Institutional Shareholding)+b10 (Firm-PSU)+b11

(Firm-MNC)+b12 (In (Sales)) + e

A similar model for the ratio of variable to total pay of the CEO would be:

Variable Component of Compensation/Total Compensation =

a+b1 (NPM)+b2 (ROA)+b4 (INC ROA)

+b5 (TRS)I + b6 (CEO-Chairman) + b7(CEO-Promoter)

+b8 (Per cent Independent Directors)

+b9 (Per cent Institutional Shareholding)+ b10 (Firm-PSU)

+b11 (Firm-MNC)+b12 [In (Sales)] + e

The Data

The primary source of our data comes form the electronic database Capitaline. It is a large repository of financial and non-financial information of more than 10,000 Indian companies. It contains detailed time series information on the financial performance of various companies along with company specific information including the digital formats of the annual reports filed by companies. Apart from this database, the other sources used included the annual reports of companies available at the specific company websites and the website of the National Stock Exchange. These sources were used to either cross check certain data points obtained from Capitaline or to obtain data that was missing. PROWESS, the corporate database of the Center for Monitoring of the Indian Economy (CMIE) was used to obtain data on stock prices.

Since this is a cross sectional study of executive compensation the compensation data and other independent/control variables covers a single time period: we use the last complete financial years for each company. Most Indian companies have their financial years running from April 1 to the March 31 of the following year. For these companies the financial year April 2004 to March 2005 is considered. Other companies having financial years ending at different points like December 2004 or June 2005 were also present in the data set. All data related to compensation, firm performance and corporate governance was valid as on the last date of each company's financial year (March 31, 2005, December 31, 2004, June 30, 2005, etc, as the case maybe).

A cross sectional study like this one needs a fairly

large data set to establish the correlations between the various parameters put forth in the model. The data in the sample must also capture the variations in the values of the independent variables and should also consists of firms for which data on CEO compensation, financial results and other firm characteristics needed by the regression model are easily available. Hence, the data set will be limited to the universe of public limited companies that are traded on stock exchanges. For this study, companies whose stocks are a part of the BSE 500 index were chosen. The BSE 500 index is a wide-ranging index consisting of a basket of 500 stocks that are listed and traded on the Bombay Stock Exchange. The BSE 500 index represents almost 93 per cent represents almost 93 per cent of the total market capitalisation of stocks listed on the BSE. It is considered to be an index that very closely represents the total secondary market. It consists of the stocks of firms in all the major industries in India. The index also has considerable variation in the size of the representative companies. Hence, companies that are part of this index are suitable for use in this study.

Out of the set of companies belonging to the BSE 500 index, only companies that disclose data on executive compensation for their last financial year can be included in the data set. On examining the data of the companies, it was found that a number of companies were not disclosing data on executive compensation. They had to be excluded from the data set. In the end, 409 companies belonging to the BSE 500 index found their way into the data set, with the other companies being excluded for lack of data.

Data on firm performance measures like NPM, ROA and incremental NPM and ROA was obtained from the annual income and balance sheet statements of each company available in Capitaline. The Latter also contains the historical records of dividends announced by the company in each financial year.

Capitaline also yielded information on the firm characteristics used in the model. Data on the sales or revenue of each company was obtained from the profit and loss statement for the corresponding financial year. The database also maintains a classification companies based on ownership types. This was used to identify the PSUs and MNCs in the data set.

Data on the corporate governance parameters was obtained from the corporate governance reports that are filed by companies as part of their annual reports. The corporate governance reports contain detailed information about the composition and functioning of the board of directors. The report lists out the profiles of the members of the board and their status, thereby identifying the independent directors. The number of independent directors and the total number of directors was thus obtained. The report also contains the designations and the responsibilities of each member of the board who is an executive director. From the classification, the CEO and chairman of the board where identified. Similarly, companies also disclose which of their directors belong to the promoter group. From this information the CEOs who belonged to the promoter group were identified as the owner managers in the sample.

The extent of institutional shareholding in the company was obtained from the shareholding pattern report that companies need to disclose in the annual report. The data that was obtained from the annual reports of companies was also cross checked with the filings made by the company to the stock exchanges (obtained at the NSE website).

The most important part of the data collecting process was to find out the compensation level and structure for the CEO of every company. In the first step, the CEO of the company had to be identified. The director occupying the highest executive position on the board was identified as the CEO.

The data on CEO compensation was obtained from two sources. The section of the corporate governance report dealing with the functioning of the remuneration committee of the board was one such source where in detailed information was available about the compensation contracts of the executive directors of the board. For some companies, data on compensation was available in the disclosed made in the annual report on employee remuneration as per Section 217 of the Companies Act, 1956.

The total amount of compensation paid to the CEO was considered to be the sum of all components of pay that were disclosed in the annual report. This usually includes the basic salary, house rent, monetary value of perquisites, sitting fees, contribution to retirement fund, performance pay, etc. However, the grant of stock options was excluded when calculating the total CEO compensation. Another important piece information collected was the variable component of CEO pay. A variable component is assumed to be performance-linked thereby "incentivising" the CEO to work for shareholder interests. All the performance-linked components of the CEO's compensation is assumed to be variable pay. Common names used by companies for variable pay include performance-linked payment, bonus, commission on profits, etc. So any pay that was mentioned under these headings was included as pat of variable pay.

Results Determinants of Total CEO Pay

The OLS regression results of total CEO pay is presented. It was hypothesised that measures of profitability and total CEO pay would be positively associated (Hypotheses). However, the results show that none of the profitability measures can significantly explain the variation in total CEO pay across firms. This is in contrast to the earlier studies of Ramaswamy et al (2000) and Ghosh (2003) where current year's ROA was found to be a significant determinant of total CEO compensation.

In contrast to Hypothesis the returns to shareholders, TRS, exhibits a small negative relationship to total CEO pay. However, the relationship is not statistically significant.

Earlier studies on compensation of CEOs in Indian firms have reported contrasting results on the effect of firm size. While Ramaswamy et al (2002) reported that firms size was not a significant explanatory variable, Ghosh (2003) concluded that firm size was indeed a very significant variable in explaining CEO compensation. The results in clearly show that firm size [measured in terms of log (sales)] has a positive and very significant (at the 0.001 level) effect on total CEO pay. Hence, Hypothesis is accepted.

The dummy variable Comp PSU also shows a strong

negative and significant (at the 0.001 level) relationship with total CEO pay. This is in line with Hypothesis. The results imply that ceteris paribus, a CEO of a non-PSU firm receives close to seven times the total pay of a CEO belonging to a PSU.

It was also hypothesis that firms that are MNCs would pay their CEOs significant higher when compared to non-MNC firms (Hypothesis). However, the results indicate a very small positive relationship that is not statistically significant. It could be that non-MNC firms in this sample have considerably raised their CEO salaries during the last few years.

From the set of corporate governance variables, CEO-Promoter and InstituHolding were found to be statistically significant. The positive relationship between total CEO pay and the presence of a CEO who is also an owner is in line with Hypothesis. However, the predicted direction of relationship between CEO pay and extent of institutional shareholding (Hypothesis) is opposite to that obtained in the results. This positive relationship between institutional shareholding and CEO pay may be hard to explain. The results do indicate that the monitoring role of large institutional shareholders is either absent or very weak.

The proportion of independent directors on the board is not a statistically significant variable in explaining CEO pay. Ghosh (2003) concluded that the proportion of non-executive directors was a significant determinant of CEO pay. But there was no distinction made between independent directors and non-executive directors.

The results also show that a dual leadership

structure, represented by the variable CEO Chairman, has a positive relationship (as per Hypothesis) but the relationship is not statistically significant [in contrast to Ghosh 2003].

Determinants of Ratio of Variable to Total CEO Pay

The data set used in this study consisted of companies that did not disclose details about the break-up of compensation paid top their CEOs in terms of fixed and variable components. The data from these companies was used only for regressing total CEO pay in terms of all the independent variables. To establish the determinants of the proportion of total CEO pay that is variable or incentive in nature, only those companies that provided the full break-up of the total compensation paid to the CEO were included. Out of the total of 409 companies, 374 companies fitted this description. This set of 374 companies also included companies that did not pay any variable or incentive pay. Another data set consisting of those companies whose compensation included some component of variable pay (non-zero variable pay) was created. This data set consisted of 221 companies. Two separate regressions were run using these two data sets (with the same set of independent variables as before).

Column 1 contains the regression results using the entire data set of companies that disclosed the break-up of compensation (i.e., 374 companies). Column 2 contains results with the truncated sample of 221 companies whose compensation contains some amount of variable pay.

The dummy variables CEO-Promoter and Comp

PSU are strong and very significant determinants of the percentage of total CEO pay that is variable. The results show that ceteris paribus, the percentage of variable to total pay for a CEO who is also a promoter of a company is 13.57 percentage points (11.776 percentage points for the truncated data set) higher when compared to a CEO who is not. For the case of PSUs, ceteris paribus, the variable component of the total compensation of the CEO is 21.667 percentage points (25.03 percentage points for the truncated data set) lower compared to that of a CEO belonging to a non-PSU firm. These results taken together therefore validate Hypotheses.

The results also show that firm size is positively and significantly related to the proportion of variable pay. This would imply that larger firms pay a greater amount of compensation as variable pay. However, it can be seen that in case of the truncated data set, firm size becomes significant only at the 0.1 level (compared to the 0.001 level using the complete data set). This may be due to the fact that the truncated data set may already contain the larger sized forms with lesser variation in firm size when compared to the complete data set.

The dummy variable CompMNC exhibits a negative association with the proportion of variable pay in the results of both regressions. The relationship is significant (at the 0.1 level) in the regression using the truncated data set. This is in contrast to what was hypothesized (Hypothesis) earlier. As before, it could be than non-MNC firms in recent years have considerably increased the variable component of their CEO pay.

The dummy variable CEO-chairman that represents the dual leadership structure of the board is also positively related to the proportion of variable pay of the CEO (Hypothesis). It is found to be a significant variable when using the truncated data set (at the 0.1 level). The result indicates that ceteris paribus, a CEO who also occupies the position of the chairman will receive a greater proportion of variable pay, to the extent of 6.33 percentage points, when compared to a CEO who is not the chairman of the board.

Conclusions

It was proposed that CEO compensation was a function of three distinct sets of parameters: firm performance and shareholder wealth, firm specific characteristics and corporate governance parameters. This was done because the issue of executive compensation is fundamentally complex with a number of diverse factors playing a role.

The results obtained show that none of the profitability measures is a significant determinant of total CEO pay. Firm size is a significant variable in explaining both total CEO pay and the proportion of variable or incentive pay that a CEO receives. We also found that CEOs who are promoters or owners receive compensation that is higher and with a greater incentive component compared to other CEOs. This study also provides evidence that CEOs of PSUs are significantly underpaid when compared to their counterparts in other firms.

Thus paper therefore adds compared to the limited empirical literature available on the determinants of executive compensation in Indian firms. The few studies that exist [Ramaswamy et al 2000; Ghosh 2003] used data that are quite dated and narrowly focused on firms belonged to certain industries. The data used in this paper is large and encompasses to entire range of industries that are found in the Indian corporate sector. This study also uses data that belongs to the latest time period for which information on firm performance, corporate governance and executive compensation is available to researchers. The effects of the changes regulatory framework surrounding corporate governance are all captured in this study.

3

Productivity in Indian Chemical Sector: An Intra-Sectoral Analysis

There are increasing number of studies on factor productivity growth in both developed and developing countries. It was Abramovitz (1957) measured total factor productivity (TFP) as a shift in the production function. Since then there has been increasing number of studies on TFP. Productivity growth is a crucial factor in determining growth of an economy. The study of productivity becomes imperative in view of the limited availability of factors of production, particularly capital. Productivity is the marginal contribution of a factor to the output growth of a product. The proportion of factors of inputs will be different in different industries. In the labour-intensive industries, the emphasis is on the capital productivity. On the other hand, for the capital-intensive industries, the concern is to increase labour productivity. If productivity is increasing in an economy it means that its factors of production and commodity inputs are manifesting an increase in their output efficiency. The productivity improvements along with the increase in the quantities of factors will also be contributing an additional source of output increase [Brahmananda 1982]. Productivity growth is necessary not only to increase output, but also to enhance the competitiveness for an industry both in the domestic and international markets. Besides, productivity growth enhances the export competitiveness of a country. The estimation of factor productivity will be very useful to evaluate the variations in the performance of an industry over a period of time. The prosperity of new developed nations has been attributed mainly to the sustained growth of their total factor productivity [Prescott 1997].

The process of liberalisation can be linked to the manufacturing productivity. The Indian government started to implement a wide range of economic reforms on various fronts to make domestic industries more efficient and internationally competitive. Indian firms were expected to respond positively to these measures. The liberalisation process was to expose firms to international competition and force them to introduce new methods of production, import quality inputs, capital equipment or technology and compel them to improve their efficiency.

Indian firms experienced the reform process since 1991 and we now have enough data to estimate the impact of globalization and liberalisation policies on Indian industry. There are mixed results revealed by earlier studies. Majumdar (1996) and Sharma (1999) estimated positive impact of liberalisation policies on the factor productivity. But Balakrishnan et al (2002) and Das (2004) found the trade liberalisation did not yield to the productivity growth in the Indian manufacturing sector. The earlier studies were conducted for the aggregates of an industry behave alike and therefore industry level characteristics could be attributed to all the firms operating in that industry. But Siddharthan (2004) argues that during the period of liberalisation, new firms with more advanced technologies are likely to enter into industry and the existing firms are expected to develop a strategy to meet the challenges from the new entrants, in particular multinational enterprises (MNEs). Under such a situation, the assumption of homogeneity becomes invalid.

It is found from the earlier studies that all the firms belonging to one industry do not behave in a similar pattern. In an industry consisting of a variety of firms with significant differences in their size, ownership, knowledge and access to technology, the liberalisation process would result in gainers and losers and there will be a productivity gap among firms in an industry. In is in this context that the present study attempts to estimate the trends in the growth of total factor productivity of Indian chemical industries at the sub-sectoral level. The Indian chemical industry consists of five major sectors, namely, *(a)* fertilizer, *(b)* drugs and pharmaceuticals, *(c)* basic chemicals, *(d)* paints and varnishes, and *(e)* dyes and dyestuffs. The study proceeds to estimate the productivity variations in these sub-sectors at the sectoral and firm level caused by the liberalisation process. This paper is divided into the following sections: Section I provided the data and methodology, Section II estimates factor productivity growth at the sectoral level. Sectoral III deals with productivity differentials at firm level and

Section IV presents summary and conclusion.

Data and Methodology

This paper covers a period of 22 years from 1980-81 to 2001-02. The entire period is divided into two phases as perform period (1980-81 to 1990-91) and post-reform period (1991-92 to 2001-02). Such a classification of the study period is essential to find the impact of economic reforms on the improvements of factor productivity. This paper attempts to estimate the total factor productivity of chemical industries in India at the sub-sectoral level. The estimation of productivity at the aggregate, sub-sectoral and firm level will reveal the performance of this industry and the homogeneity of the subsectors in relation to the liberalisation process.

Description of Data and Variables

The present study is based on the unpublished firm level data on the public limited chemical industries obtained from the Company Finances Division of the Reserve Bank of India (RBI). Various studies have used RBI firm level data in their analysis Srivastava 1996; [Feingberg and Majumdar 2001]. The study is made for the five major sub-sectors of the Indian chemical sector, viz, fertilizer, drugs and pharmaceuticals, basic chemicals, paints and varnishes and dyes and dyestuffs. These sub-sectors together constitute nearly 71 per cent of the total chemical sector in India (as per the RBI data in 2001-02). According to the industry codes given by the RBI, the value of each variable was summed up for each sub-sector for the period under consideration. The gross value of production has been taken as a measure of output. Generally, the TFP growth estimates based on value added terms are overestimated as they ignore the contribution of intermediate inputs on productivity growth [Sharma 1999], hence a third variable of intermediate inputs (consumption of raw materials) has been included in the function. Pradhan and Barik (1999) argued that the output, instead of value added, appears to be the appropriate choice of TFPG estimation in India. To offset the influence of price changes, output was deflated by the wholesale price index (1980-81 = 100) of the corresponding sub-sectors and the raw materials by the WPI of intermediate goods with the same base. The total number of workers and the gross fixed asset are considered measures of labour and capital inputs. Gross fixed capital was deflated by the WPI of machinery and machine products (base 1980-81=100), thus the real gross fixed capital was included in the function. Since the RBI does not publish the employment details, the average wage rate of the industry was calculated from the Annual Survey of Industries (ASI) data for all the years of the study. The average wage rate was estimated by dividing the total emolument of the industry by the number of workers in that industry [Goldar and other 2004]. This average wage rate obtained from the ASI data was then used to divide the total wages and salary of each sub-sector to estimate the number of workers at the sub-sectoral level. Further the size of the firm is determined on the basis of number of workers. From the data set of RBI, the firms which were present during the entire period of study were separated and grouped as small and large firms. Since there are some differences in size distribution across sectors, the firms are defined "small" ("large") when the level of employment is less (more) than the geometric mean level of employment of the sector in which the firm operates [Sak and Taymaz 2004].

Estimates of Factor Productivity Growth

Factor productivity growth rates are computed for the five major sub-sectors of Indian chemical industries. Theoretically there appears to be a relationship between policy measures and productivity growth, although the empirical findings for some developing countries are ambivated. Ahluwalia (1985, 1991) and Parades (1994) found a significant improvement in the productivity growth while Kajiwara (1994) for Philippines and Urata and Yokota for Thailand (1994) estimated a fall in the manufacturing productivity following liberalisation. The estimated annual and mean growth rates of TFP. Wide variations in the magnitude of TFPG are found in the estimation. The estimated TFPG of the Indian chemical sector at the aggregate and sub-sectoral level reveals contradictory rates of productivity growth. The fertiliser industry recorded positive rates of TFP throughout the study period except during 1991-92 (-1.327) and 1997-98 (-0-022). As against this, the drugs and pharmaceutical industry recorded negative productivity growth rates except in 1999-2000, 2000-2001 and 2001-2002. During these periods there were positive growth rates of total factor productivity. The basic chemical industries registered positive and negative productivity growth rates both in the pre- and post-reform periods. Paints and varnishes industry have positive TFPG in 1986-87 (1.084), 1997-98 (0.156) and in 2001-02 (0.005). But the dyes and dyestuff industries have experienced positive TFPG mostly in the post-reform period. At aggregate level also the negative trend in the TFPG is observed during the period of study. Pradhan and Barik (1999) are of the view that the low and negative trend in the TFPG is a common feature in most of the developing countries. They also estimated a negative TFPG for the Indian chemical sector in their study. From this analysis, it could be observed that the impact of the reform process is mixed even within a particular sector.

In order to understand the influence of economic reforms on TFPG, the mean growth rates of TFP were estimated for the pre- and post-reform period and are presented. The estimated mean TFPG for the aggregate and the sub-sectors of the Indian chemical industry reveal a contradictory picture with the positive and negative rates. For the period 1980-81 to 2001-02, the mean TFPG was positive for fertilizers (0.847) and dyes and dyestuff (0.016) while it was negative for drugs and pharmaceuticals (-0.175), basic chemicals (-0.126) and for paints and varnishes, it was –0.490. At the aggregate level, the TFPG was also negative at –0.199 during this period.

During the pre-reform period (1980-81 to 1990-91), invariably all the major sub-sectors have recorded negative TFPG except the fertiliser industry with a positive productivity rate of 0.903. The negative rates varied among the other sectors, viz, drugs, and pharmaceuticals (-0.234), basic chemicals (-0.132), paints and varnishes (-0.819) and dyes and dyestuff industry (-0.111).

It could be noticed from the mean TFPG estimated

during the post-reform period that the reform process yielded mixed results on the productivity levels of the sub-sectors of Indian chemical sector. The economic reforms started to yield positive results in drugs and pharmaceuticals, basic chemicals and paints and varnishes industries. It is visible from the estimated mean TFPG that there is a significant drop in the extent of negative TFPG when compared to that in the pre-reform period. In the case of dyes and dyestuff industries, the negative productivity growth estimated in the pre-reform period (-0.111) has even turned out to be positively (0.144) in the post-reforms period. As against this, the impact of economic reforms was found to be negative in the case of the fertiliser industries. The mean growth rate of TEP of this sector, through positive, declined to 0.791, when compared to the pre-reform period (0.903). But at the aggregate level, the negative rate further worsened to –0.227 from –0.171 estimated in the pre-reform period. From the mean growth rates of TFP, it can be stated that the net impact of economic reforms was quite conducive to the sub-sectors of the Indian chemical industries except for the fertilizers industry. But the impact varied in its magnitude depending on the nature of the industry.

Firm Size and Productivity Differentials

The differences in productivity growth at the firm level will reveal the homogeneity/heterogeneity of a sector in an industry. Industry becomes more productive when the firms operating in the industry adopt new and better methods of production. The assumption of homogeneity of an industry holds good when all the firms in an industry tend to have a similar pattern of productivity changes. But due to the differences in its size, particularly in the changing market environment, the productivity changes tend to vary. In an open market, some firms thrive while other disappears. There are, within the industry, winners and loser. The notion is that the inefficient firms can a more competitive environment [Levinsohn and Amil 1999]. Therefore, when the economy becomes more competitive, the productivity differentials widen depending on the size of the firms operating in the industry. Indeed, there appears to be a fact that there exist productivity differentials between small and large-scale enterprises independent of the sector and economy. Gulbiten and Taymaz (2000) in their study found that there are substantial productivity differentials between small-sized enterprises and large corporations independent of sector and economy, and the productivity differentials decrease by economic development but do not vanish even in the developed countries.

Earlier studies have concluded that small firms are less productive than the large ones. The productivity differentials between small and large firms seem to originate from number of sources. You (1995) and Taymaz (2004) found that technological factors (economies of scale) are the principal determinants of such differences. Gulbiten and Taymaz (2000) explain that the small firms may be as efficient as large firms but operate less productively than the larger firms since they may not be exploiting economies of scale. Secondly, small firms may be maximizing profits with existing capital, labour and technology, yet they may be operating less productively than the larger firms because they utilize older technologies and low quality inputs. Further, the existence of wage differences may also result in productivity differentials between small and large firms. For example, small firms tend to pay lower wages than their counterparts. Although small firms seem to be advantageous in terms of labour cost they face, lower wages are usually accompanied by less skilled labourers and the disadvantage of utilizing cheap unskilled labourers might outstrip its cost advantage, reducing the small firms' productiveness.

The underlying facts of the extent of productivity differentials of small and large firms in an industry have become a measure of homogeneity of the industry concerned. Within this purview, the study has made an attempt to estimate the TFP growth of he different sub-sectors of the Indian chemical industry at the firm level during the period of study.

The presents the estimated mean TFP growth rates of small and large firms in each sub-sector of the Indian chemical industry. The obtained mean TFPG estimates show that the small firms have lower productivity growth than the large firms. Further, small firms in all the sub-sectors are found to have a lower productivity level than their sectoral mean levels of productivity estimated for the entire period of study except the paints and varnishes sector in which the TFPG of small firms is marginally higher at –0.111 than its sectoral mean rate of -0.490. On the contrary, the large firms in each sub-sector have higher rates of TFP except in the fertiliser sector where there is a marginal fall in the mean rate of TFPG of large firms at 0.755, when compared to the sectoral mean rate or 0.847.

From it can be noticed that when the chemical sector as a whole witnessed a decline in the productivity level during the post-reform period, the sub-sectors, other than fertilizers, marked an improvement. But the picture was different at the firm level. Invariably, the small firms in all the sub-sectors experienced a significant decline in productivity growth rates during the post-reform period except in the drugs and pharmaceutical sector in which they recorded a marginal improvement to –0.399 from –0.432 estimated for the pre-reform period. Urata and Kawai (2001) found that larger firms normally have higher total factor productivity levels and growth than smaller firms. There are, however, some exceptions to this pattern where small firms tend to have an edge due to two distinctive features of small firms, viz, the practice of sub-contracting and use of external patents. Whereas in the case of large firms, there was a significant improvement in the TFPG of all the sub-sectors except fertilizers in which both small and large firms experienced a decline in the productivity growth during the post-reform period. It is perhaps due to the increase in the factor inputs. Schumachar and Jayant (1999) noted that following liberalisation, output declined considerably and thereby decreased the productivity of the fertilizer industry in the country. They also found that increase in the material input was the driving factor for productivity losses in the Indian fertilizer sector.

A simple comparison of the productivity differentials between small and large firms at the sub-sectoral level reveals that both in the pre- and post-reform period, the small firms are found to productivity levels of larger ones. The higher productivity levels of large firms compared to the small firms may be due to the better exploitation of economies of scale by them. Further, the large firms are able to use high quality inputs, better technologies and make huge investment on R&D activities. As a result, they could get greater returns from their increased innovative measures. Similarly, one more argument can be put forth for the comparatively better productivity performance of large firms. The liberalisation measures have made the market environment more competitive. Under highly competitive market conditions, the small firms failed to compete while large firms could manage with the adoption of advanced technologies of production. Tybout (2000) points out a fact that there exists a discrimination of small and large firms in the financial market also. Especially in a country where private sector credit is scarce and rationed, financial institutions discriminate against small and large firms thereby increasing the cost conditions of small firms and thus decreased their productivity levels.

Findings and Conclusion

The simple analysis made to estimate the intra-industry productivity variations in the Indian chemical sector during the period 1980-81 to 2001-02 reveals contradictory results at the aggregate, sectoral and firm level. On the whole the impact of economic reforms on total factor productivity at the aggregate level was poor as the negative mean rate of TFPG estimated in the pre-reform period further increased in the post-reform period. But this declining trend is not applicable to all the sub-sectors. The estimated measures of TFPG at the sectoral level show that the TFPG of drugs and pharmaceuticals, paints and varnishes, basic chemical and dyes and dyestuff industries are better in the post-reform period as there is a change in the sign or a decline in the extent of negative productivity growth. But in the case of the fertilizer industry, the liberalisation process is found to have its adverse impact as there is a fall in the total factor productivity growth during the post-reform period. At the firm level, though the small firms in the drugs and pharmaceutical and paints and varnishes sector experienced a marginal increase in the productivity growth while large firms in the fertilizer sector market a decline during the post-reform period.

Thus, the pattern of total productivity growth showed mixed trends in the Indian chemical sector at the intra-sectoral level. To sum up, TFPG itself witnessed a better performance in the post-reform period at the sub-sectoral level which is different from the industry average. When firms size is considered, in both the periods, the small firms have lower levels of productivity growth than the larger firms. Irrespective of the sectors, the large firms, due to the better exploitation of economies of scale and the ability to adopt new methods of production, are more productive than the small ones. Tybout (2000) suggested that small firms should adopt more innovative measures to make them more efficient and productive. That is, the innovation initiated either to survive or to create their own market niches appears to be effective in increasing efficiency. With the present economic environment, these results cannot be finalized. There are time lags in the realization of the final result of the reform measures like foreign capital inflows, R&D, technology transfers and the other spillover effects exerted by the foreign entrants. One important conclusion that can be drawn from this analysis is that this study confirms the results of Liu (1993), Liu assumption of homogeneity, that is all the firms in an industry are alike, might not be valid. The variations in the growth rates and the signs prove that the heterogeneity conditions prevail in the industry and under such conditions, liberalisation would result in gainers and losers in an industry. It is suggested that while making policy decisions on the basis of aggregates, the consideration of intra-sectoral variations will provide more valuable decisions.

4

Corporate Governance Codes in India

The issue of corporate governance (CG) gained prominence with the publication of Jensen and Meckling's article (1976) which triggered a body of theoretical and empirical work on the subject. During the 1970s and 1980s, theoretical and applied research work on CG was focused primarily on US corporations. By the early 1990s similar work had been done in other developed countries such as Japan, Germany, and the United Kingdom. This was quickly followed by research in CG in emerging markets.

The debate on corporate governance in Indian thus draws heavily on Anglo-American experience, literature and practice. Indian corporate sector regulators have been quick to assimilate and apply international CG practices based on the latest available knowledge. But these practices do not necessarily signal convergence in the values embedded in our national culture. Given the manner in which Indian firms have evolved since independence, and the role that FIs have played, corporate governance issues and problems in India are different to those typically encountered abroad. Adopting international CG practices without suitable modification does not, therefore, help to address or resolve specific governance issues plaguing the behaviour of Indian firms. Issues such as the effect of ownership concentration on shareholder rights, the role of relationship-based activity between banks and non-bank corporations, its impact on creditor participation in corporate governance, the prevalence of insiders and promoters, the effect of social and corporate culture on disclosure, transparency and enforcement, etc, cannot be resolved simply by transplanting international CG practices.

India's equity markets and corporate governance structures are well developed compared to other emerging markets. Yet, they have been unable to bring about a desired change in the equality of corporate governance and firm-performance for the vast majority of listed companies. Large companies that are exposed to international markets have adopted international CG standards that are generally more rigorous than those applied in India; but these are exceptions to the norm.

The recent (2004-06) rally in the Indian stock markets– buoyed by an economic growth rate of 8 per cent and an increasing appreciation on the part of global investors of India's vast potential – drove overseas investors to buy a record $ 2.85 billion. All this helped push shares prices significantly higher for a select group of large and medium size companies. But the rest have remained impervious to international investment. In order to sustain international investors' interest in Indian markets over the long-term, and `to spread such interest across a broader spectrum of listed companies, a stronger focus on CG issues (specific to India) and how CG can be applied to all listed firms is, among other needed changes, an imperative.

Following this line of argument, this article emphasizes the relevance and importance of CG for India. It considers how Indian CG standards compare with international standards in letter and spirit, pointing out areas where espousal of international practices has made little difference and why those areas remain a challenge for the inculcation of good CG in India. The first section of this article briefly describes what corporate governance is, the importance of CG in general, as well as more specifically in India. The second section deals with the structural features of the Indian economy which have contributed to sticky corporate practices detriment to the objective of good governance. The third section illustrates how Indian CG codes compare with international standards and codes. In concluding, the article deals with issues that pose challenges to good corporate governance in India.

What is Corporate Governance?

Issues of CG arise because of the separation of ownership from management and control in modern corporations. In economic parlance, CG issues arise wherever contracts are incomplete and agency problems exists. Given this separation of ownership from control and the involvement of stakeholders, CG concerns the way in which other shareholders and stakeholders can legitimately exercise influence and exert effective control over the actions of corporate managers/promoters. The discipline of corporate governance has developed as a way of ensuring that: *(a)* investors other than promoters receive a fair return on their investment by protecting them against management expropriation or use of the investment capital to finance poor projects and *(b)* other stakeholders are assured that their interests are properly catered for. CG is a system by which firms are directed and monitored.

Definitions of corporate governance vary widely. They tend to fall into two categories. The first set of definitions concerns itself within a set of behavioural patterns: that is, the actual behaviour of corporations, in terms of such measures as performance, efficiency, growth, financial structure, and treatment of shareholders and other stakeholders. The second set concerns itself with the normative framework for governance: i e, the rules under sources like the legal system, the judicial system, financial markets, and factor (labour) markets. A comprehensive definition of corporate governance suggests that it is "the complex set of constraints the shape ex post bargaining over the quasi rents generated by the firm" which focuses on the division of claims. Following from that logic, CG is the complex set of constraints that determine quasi-rents (profits) generated by the firm in the course of relationships and shape ex post bargaining over them. This definition refers to both the determination of value-addition by firms and the allocation or sharing of such value among stakeholders that have legitimate relationships with the firm.

Importance of CG

Worldwide the "corporation" is considered to be the essential engine driving the private sector economically. CG is critical to its competitive performance. CG is of particular importance at a time when interactions between companies and their capital suppliers are undergoing fundamental changes. Due to global deregulation and technological change, entrepreneurs and companies are exposed to a wider and more complete range of capital-raising vehicles. For corporations, this means that they can support a variety of R&D activities, spin-offs, capacity expansion and new firm creation. Greater competition for capital results in greater pressure for corporate economic performance and significant pressures on long-standing relationships with employees. Failure to adopt to efficient governance practices any well lead to restricted access to capital markets. On the other hand, globalization means capital suppliers are encountering new opportunities to improve their returns. They are willing to provided capital when they are confident that their growth rest on secure foundations. Research shows that in both OECD and emerging market countries, well-governed companies attract premium valuations. Better corporate governance standards make banks and rating agencies see companies in a better light. This means lower borrowing costs for well-governed firms.

CG plays a critical role at every stage of the investment process At the first stage in the investment process, effective property protection and secure methods of ownership registration are basic corporate governance provisions that influence a firm's ability to mobilize capital. At the second stage, reliable and transparent disclosure is essential if the market it to allocate available funds the procedures for corporate decision-making, the distribution of authority among company organs, and the design of incentive schemes are examples of governance arrangement that have to be in place to effectively monitor the capital that is handed over to firms.

By demanding transparency in corporate transactions, in accounting and auditing procedures, and in all business transactions generally. CG attacks the supply side of the corruption relationship, especially in developing countries. Government helps to provide legitimacy for governments undertaking unpopular reforms by indicating to the public that the government is not merely cutting back on welfare spending, but is developing an effective corporate structure which will generate conditions for further growth. CG is important greater efficiency among domestic firms to compete with MNSc in unprotected markets.

CG in India

In spite of the fact that adoption of the international CG practices has made little difference in India, CG still has the potential to play a very important role in India's long-run and sustainable economic growth. India effectively began its move towards a more open and market friendly economy in 1991. Since liberalization, India has seen a spectacular growth in the size of its stock markets, i.e., number of firms listed and the value of the shares listed or the market capitalization. The importance of CG is reflected in the growth that Indian stock markets have made in the last decade. During the capital market boom of 1993-95, many companies that tapped the capital market for funds defaulted in their commitments and simply vanished. Hundreds of obscure companies made public issues at large premia, with the help of obscure investment banks and misleading prospectuses. The managements of these companies siphoned off more than $ 2.2 billion, saddling around 11 million small investors with illiquid stocks of defunct companies. Moreover, the continued preponderance of firms with very low market capitalization (around 80 per cent of the total listed companies) reflects a deep-rooted structural flaw in Indian capital markets. Too many of these cases represent outright fraud and inefficiency; they call for effective external and internal CG mechanisms.

Liberalization and its associated developments, i.e., deregulation, privatization, internal and external liberalization of product markets as well as extensive financial liberalization, have made effective corporate governance more crucial. These developments have meant that the availability of long-term funds to firms from development finance institutions (mostly state-controlled) has declined markedly in the past decade when the need for extra-firm finance has increased substantially. The supply of extra-firm fiancé is now fulfilled mainly by capital markets and by syndicated loans from commercial banks. Cases of fraud, corruption (on the part of regulators), market manipulation (on the part of securities companies, brokers) and other malpractices (on the part of firms) in the equity market can render capital market reforms desultory and lead to low investors confidence. Fraudulent companies usually crowd out public investment from equity markets and the victims of general investor apathy are "genuine" companies. Firms with poor governance are forced to finance operations and growth internally to a much greater extent. This situation can become particularly detrimental for smaller firms and pose a serious development trap in which firms find it difficult to fund their investment projects as financial institutions have atrophied in importance and capital markets have become inefficient. Independent and effective corporate governance institutions thus become necessary in order to restore the credibility of capital markets to facilitate the flow of investment finance to firms. International creditors are also increasingly evaluating companies on the basis of these criteria-commitment to good CG, shareholder rights, BoD, transparency and disclosure.

A good system of corporate governance in India has long being recognized as important for the domestic economy, in that it can raise efficiency and growth; particularly when stock markets are playing an increasingly significant role in financing investment. CG has implications for the functioning of the Indian financial system in terms of: better allocation of capital over time; the ability of Indian firms to raise funds overseas and compete internationally, reducing the likelihood of a domestic financial crisis as well as an external payments crisis; and laying a strong foundation for further opening of the capital account. As India embarks on a high growth trajectory, larger current account deficits will come about, an effective CG system will ensure that these larger current account deficits can be financed with longer-term and less speculative funds, reducing the chances of an external crisis in the future, even as capital inflows increase and remaining capital account restrictions are slowly phased out. The next section deals with some structural features related financial and legal systems of the economy which have contributed the poor CG practices in India.

Structural Characteristics

India withstood the Asian financial crisis of 1997-98 comparatively well, but the fallout from the crisis demonstrated that the corporate sector could play an important role in transmitting financial shocks and putting the financial sector at risk. Mis-matches in the corporate sector's balance sheet brought to light both domestic and external vulnerabilities. The Asian crisis showed that the deterioration in creditworthiness of large segments of the corporate sector sharply increases non-performing loans (NPLs), curtails new investment, and contributes to capital fight, all of which adversely affects economic activity as a whole. With a comparatively low level of foreign debt as a source of funds and India's strong foreign exchange risk is low as this point of time. Other than this, only good CG practices can help an economy to withstand such systemic crises.

India's corporate sector has growth steadily over the past two decades in terms of number of registered companies and amount of paid up capital. The corporate sector consists of closely held (private limited) and publicly held (public limited) companies, with approximately 6,19,000 registered companies in 2004, about 40 per cent of which are in the manufacturing sector. Private limited companies comprise the majority of firms in the corporate sector, but account for less than one-third of the total paid-up capital. Government-owned enterprises (both public and private limited) are comparatively few in number but large in size, accounting for more than 25 per cent of the paid-up capital.

The ownership of India's corporate sector tends to be concentrated in the hands of firm promoters and, to a lesser extent, small investors. Focusing on the manufacturing sector, promoters' share was 48 per cent of the paid-up capital for all companies in 2002 and as high as 71 per cent for government-owned enterprises. The prevalence of cross-holdings of ownership, together with heavy owner participation, makes India's system of corporate control close to an "insider" one. The share of equity held by small (public) investors in India (32 per cent) is comparable to that of the US and UK (countries with a pronounced "outsider" system), inter-corporate holdings in India are much higher. In addition, financial institutions (FIs) in India hold a much smaller share of equity as compared to other countries and have been characterized as largely passive shareholders, mostly supportive of managements' positions. In the Indian business groups, the concept of dominant shareholders is unstructured for two reasons. First, the promoters' shareholding is spread across several friends and relatives as well as corporate entities. It is sometimes difficult to establish the total effective holding of this group. Second, the aggregate holding of all these entities taken together is typically well below a majority stake. In may cases, the promoter may not even be the largest single shareholder. What makes the promoters the dominant shareholders is that a large chunk of the shares is held by state owned financial institutions which have historically played a passive role.

The major DFIs in India played a significant role in funding corporate growth, during a period when equity markets had not evolved to their current dominant status. However, FIs did very little to monitor their firms, until it was too late. Even in the presence of signs of financial distress in firms, FIs made available more funds to cover losses, thus further increasing their debt-equity ratios. Until 1991, the objective of financial policy in India was to maximize loans for industrial development without adequate regard to recovery and monitoring. FIs were lax in their duty of corporate monitoring because the government did not desire that any of the existing managements ignoring their dual interests as debt and shareholders. FIs rarely divested their shareholding and legal institutions provided promoters with preferential rights (irrespective of corporate performance) helping them to hold on to their shareholding.

The legal framework governing Indian corporate sector is based on common law. Firms are governed by the Companies Act (CA), 1956 as amended. The CA is administered by the Department of Company Affairs (DCA) and enforced by the Company Law Board (CLB) and the company courts. Listed companies must comply with the rules and regulations prescribed by the Securities and Exchange Board of India (SEBI) Act, 1992; with the Securities Contract (Regulation) Act, 1956; the Depositories Act, 1996; the Sick Industrial Companies (special Provisions) Act (SICA), 1985; and the listing rules. Changes in the legal and regulatory framework in the post-1991 period have been key to promoting greater competition, reducing the regulatory burden, and, of late, strengthening corporative governance, which will continue to be of crucial importance to India's growth prospects.

Other structural feature of the Indian economy is concerned with bankruptcy and liquidation laws and procedures. These are inadequate, time consuming and contribute to poor governance by management. Bankruptcy reorganization of large industrial organisations of large industrial organisations is governed by the Sick Industrial Companies (Special Provisions) Act, 1985 and the process is supervised by the Board for Industrial and Financial Reconstruction (BIFR). The latter tends to support the rights of existing management and of old shareholders over fully secured creditors. Liquidation poses even more serious problems. This is because most liquidation cases take between one to two decades to complete in the Indian courts, resulting in a system that works against the interests of workers and secured creditors. Since management fears neither attachment nor bankruptcy, it leads to companies funding highly risky investments, which has several adverse consequences. It raises the cost of credit, it debases the disciplining role of debt and it increasingly risks the health of the financial sector. Probably the principal reason is that the major banks and mutual funds are under the control of the government. They are buffeted by contradictory pulls by the various ministries and therefore have difficulty in focusing on commercial accountability. The government involvement also raises the moral hazard problem with the financial institutions exposing themselves to risky lending and activities, because they known that they will be bailed out by the government, if they run into difficulties. These features are quintessential of an inability to cede control and of shirking from responsibility. The following two sections deal with the international codes of CG and how India measures up to these practices.

International Standards and Codes of CG

Good corporate governance systems are rooted in an appropriate combination of legal protection of investors and some form of concentrated ownership. The US and UK systems rely more heavily on stronger legal protection, while the German and Japanese systems are characterized by the more concentrated equity ownership.

An observer of the international governance scene commented that if corporate governance codes appeared in trade figures, Britain would have a far healthier balance of payments. The comment reflected the fact that the first corporate governance code of the modern era – that was instituted in the UK by the Bank of England and London Stock Exchange in 1992, and chaired by Sir Adrian Cadbury – spawned many imitators. Some of those codes are the Bosch Report, Australia (1995), the Cardon Report, Belgium (1998), the Dey Report, Canada (1994), the Vineot Report, France (1999), the King Report, South Africa (1994), the Peters Committee, Netherlands (1997), the Corporate Governance Forum of Japan, (1998), the Governance of Spanish Companies, (1998), the Swedish Academy Report, (1994), the German Panel on Corporate Governance, (2000), the Sarbanes-Oxley Report, US (2002), etc. At the multilateral level, efforts to improve CG by establishing international standards were spearheaded by the WTO and its member countries to develop standards that sought to help firms expand across national boundaries. International accounting bodies and national associations of accountants have worked to develop an international set of accounting standards. In addition, the World Bank, the OECD, most of the regional development banks, the UN and other national development agencies have either launched or expanded CG programmes. There are now more than 60 governance codes in 30 markets, numerous international codes, a vast number of individual governance or voting guidelines produced by individual investment institutions as well as industry codes. The core content of most of these codes can be broadly classified into three areas: *(i)* the independence of the board, *(ii)* the responsibilities of institutional investors or shareholders, and *(iii)* the transparency of business structure and operation.

The Cadbury Committee was based on a formula for governance that has become the industry standard– it developed a list of "best practice" governance standards to which companies were encouraged to aspire. Companies were then required to disclose how they measured up to the code, giving explanations for any areas of non-compliance. Its formula eschewed burdensome regulation or inflexible legislation; allowed companies to be free to develop their own governance practices; and, via disclosure, put the responsibility for improvement on investors.

Despite different starting points, a trend towards convergence of corporate governance regimes has been developing in recent years. This has happened due to firms adapting and adjusting as a result of the increasing globalization and integration of capital markets, the increasing exposure of policy-markers to regional and global policy for a, and the impact of those on the minds of leaders to reform is more intense now. Developing countries are increasingly adopting the Anglo-American model because: *(a)* many of these countries had historical ties with the Anglo-American model (their company law is firmly rooted in British company law) and *(b)* the apparent lack of success of previous interventionist regimes which had some elements associated with other corporate governance models. International financial institutions have also encouraged developing countries to adopt the Anglo-American model.

Although capital market pressures are driving convergence on common governance principles, international agreement on a single model of corporate governance, or a single set of detailed governance rules, is both unlikely and unnecessary. Economists agree that there cannot be a "one size fits all" standard as unfamiliar practices cannot be transplanted or imposed, and because individual companies and markets are always subject to local cultures, pressures and practices. Furthermore, achieving good CG generally is more exigent in emerging markets than in advanced economies for a number of reasons: corporate ownership in emerging economies tends to be highly concentrated, often in a few families, with only limited ownership by minority shareholders, takeover markets are thin or non-existent, regulatory inefficiencies, lack of judicial enforcement lack of property rights, contract violations, asset- stripping and self-dealing, etc. In reality, the rules-on-books regarding CG appear to be converging in response to the pressures of global competition; but convergence of actual CG practices is much slower in materializing.

Nevertheless a set of universal guiding principles are relevant especially to transitional and multinationals and multinationals. In terms of the functioning of transnational and the importance of regulatory convergence becomes critical, when countries have different company codes, capital market requirements and enforcement capabilities which transnationals can use to their advantage to arbitrage. The first effort to offer a global set of principles was done by the OECD by attempting to harmonies practices across its 29 country members, ranging from the US to South Korea.

Indian vs International CG Standards

In India the legal framework for regulation all corporate activities including governance and administration of companies, disclosures, and shareholders' rights has been in place since the enactment of Companies Act in 1956. India can be considered to be in the "post-transition regime" with a well-defined and stable corporate governance structure and where the management of enterprises is through de process defined by corporate law.

The Securities and Exchange Board of India (SEBI), an independent quasi-judicial, regulatory body, regulates the stock exchanges. Corporate governance requirements in India are largely based on recommendations of the Cadbury and Higgs Reports and the Sarbanes-Oxley Act. SEBI has been proactive in keeping India's corporate governance rules and regulations in line with best practices around the world. In 1999, SEBI appointed the Kumar Mangalam Birla

Committee to recommend improvements its listing requirements with Clause 49. These listing requirements were again changed in 2004 to incorporate some best practices laid out in the Sarbanes-Oxley Act. SEBI has also issued regulations relating to the acquisition of significant shareholdings, takeovers, share buy-backs and insider trading. Bankruptcy and anti-competitive laws are also in place. There is currently a bill in Parliament to revamp the Companies Act of 1956, which was amended as recently as 2002.

All listed companies were required to be in compliance with Clause 49 by December 31, 2005. Companies are required to provide information regarding their governance practices in a separate Corporate Governance section in the annual report to shareholders in which non-compliance with any mandatory requirements, and the extent to which non-mandatory requirements have been adopted, should be highlighted. Clause 49 also requires companies to file a quarterly compliance report with the stock exchange. The stock exchange in turn is required to file an annual compliance report with SEBI for each listed company.

The accompanying table highlights some of the differences between International CG codes and the existing Indian CG codes. All divergences from international best practices are associated to the unique structural characteristics of the Indian economy as highlighted in the table.

Challenges to Promoting Good CG

The challenges to promoting a good CG culture in India faces problems at two distinct levels i.e., at the firm level and at the macro or extra-firm level. These follow from the non-conducive structural features of the Indian economy. At the firm level, the most striking and commonly agreed failures of CG practices in India have been the widely perceived *(a)* ownership structure in companies, *(b)* failure of boars, *(c)* accounting practices and transparency.

Ownership Structure in Companies

In the private sector, most large Indian companies are a hybrid of family-owned conglomerates and publicly listed companies. Indian conglomerates have been successful in competing against multinational corporations by streamlining costs and rationalizing businesses. However, the broader corporate governance structure in Indian companies generally remains poor. The endemic features of these conglomerates are: ownership and management are not segmented, there is informality of governance policies and inadequate controls, the ownership structure of individual companies within the conglomerates is usually opaque, often the controlling family retains control by creating complex crossholdings among subsidiaries, related-party transactions among subsidiaries and, in particular, related lending is opaque. Ownership of Indian family controlled companies is now moving into the second or third generation. It is therefore imperative that further reforms need to address the specific concerns facing the family-owned conglomerate structure. It is important that, among other things, family-owned companies focus on; voluntarily adopting mechanisms for governance of the family's ownership stake; for example, crating family councils that deal with family disputes, reforming company boards by increasing overall board independence and reducing the number of family member-directors; limiting the role of family members in senior management and increasing transparency around the ownership structure and related-party transactions.

Failure of Boards

Boards in ndia do not exist as institutions of governance and truly independent directors are rare in Indian companies. There is a lack of clear understanding of what is expected from the directors in terms of their duties of care and loyalty to the company and its shareholders. In most cases therefore directors are simply for "rubber stamping" the decisions of management or promoters. Much needs to be done in terms of improvement in the constitution and functioning of the boards and their regard for minority shareholders' rights. A key missing ingredient is a strong focus on director professionalisms. In addition to the law or other regulations spelling out the responsibilities of directors, they themselves should engage in the formulation of their tasks and work procedures. The presence of FIs' nominees is the most distinctive features of Indian corporate governance system, and consequently the "failure" of corporate governance in India is often seen as failure of the FIs to safeguard the general shareholder interest. The domestic financial institutions' nominee system has been widely criticized and there has also been a strong campaign to remove nominees from boards, further reducing the accountability of boards. FIs' nominees have been criticized on the grounds that their caliber is low, their contribution is minimal, and that they lack competence to understand the nature of the business. But the FIs' nominees lack the right incentives to perform their duties with enthusiasm. There has been a constant pressure on FIs for reform of the governance culture of Indian business. Consequently, the FIs decided on radical ideas of a block sale of their equity holdings to effect a management change in the interest of a company. But this idea did not meet with much success because of a strong business lobby backlash that has chosen to make the issue of institutional nominees central to the debate on governance on the grounds that their access to price-sensitive information make institutions insiders.

Accounting Practices and Transparency

Although, FIIs have been responsible for improvements in disclosure standards, levels of disclosure remain poor, accounting standards weak, and Indian corporate structures low in transparency. In Indian the level of disclosure is abysmal and creative accounting is extensive. The greatest drawback of financial disclosures in India is the absence of detailed reporting on related party transactions. At the level of the balance sheet, there is no requirement to report which investments and loans made by the corporation are to subsidiaries and associated companies. Auditor independence is another problem because of a large and segmented market in accounting services and the perceived powerlessness of auditors in the face of corporate pressure. Chartered accountants argue that despite the absence of consolidation, Indian financial statements give enough information for analysts to reconstruct the true picture of a group of companies.; For most users of financial statements, however, the absence of consolidation, Indian financial statements give enough information for analysts to reconstruct the true picture however, the absence of consolidation leads to misrepresentation of the true picture of a business group as it does not disclose related party transactions or transactions with affiliated companies. There is also a further need for the harmonization of Indian accounting system with an internationally accepted standard like the US GAAP.

At the extra-firm level, CG problems relate to *(a)* surveillance and enforcement mechanisms and the court system, *(b)* insufficient powers of SEBI to police violations of regulations, *(c)* lack of shareholder activism in India.

Surveillance and Enforcement Mechanisms and the Court System

Although laws in India are generally comparable to those in the UK, the court system is seen as inadequate to handle the volume of cases being brought to trial. Thus results in delays in the delivery of justice. Verdicts are handed over 10 to 20 years after the incidences have occurred. Furthermore, corruption in the lower courts, delays the delivery of verdicts and increases the cost of litigation. Also, judges in lower courts who preside over murder trial are expected to be conversant with corporate law and presided over whit-collar crimes like fraud. An amendment to the Companies Act of 2002 required the establishment of special courts to handle securities and finance-related crimes. Three years after the amendment, the governance is still in the process of identifying and appointing qualified judges.

Insufficient Powers of SEBI

Despite incorporating several positive features and raising the standards in the company law, and at the level of securities market and the regulatory authority, their implementation has proven to be challenging. This is partly because SEBI has insufficient powers to police violations of regulations. Although stock exchanges in India have responsibility for surveillance, they do not have the authority to take punitive action against errant companies. Indian regulatory structure is segmented where the authority and responsibilities for surveillance and enforcement is divided among various entities, leading to a mismatch between the level of authority and responsibility. The same fate awaits a proposed bill in Parliament to revamp the Companies Act of 1956 to simplify procedures by moving to a rules-based system. When and if the bill passes, the voluminous provisions in the current act would be reduced by two-thirds from the present roughly 780 provisions. But it is unclear who will have the authority to set the rules. India's corporate governance environment is characterized by a lack of an infrastructure relating to the surveillance and enforcement mechanisms and the court system.

Shareholder Activism

In India is practically non-existent. There are several explanations for the lack of shareholder activism in the Indian equity market. In India promoters typically retain control of companies by owning a small, yet significant, ownership stake in companies. Shares not owned or controlled by the promoter and his family and friends are widely dispersed, making it difficult for minatory shareholders to voices their concerns. Although FII's increasingly own a large number shares in Indian companies, in general, no single minority shareholder owns enough shares to significantly influence change. Therefore, even though there are laws that empower shareholders controlling 10 per cent of equity, the dispersed nature of ownership of shares makes it difficult for minority shareholders to take a more active role in the management of the company. Pension and insurance companies in India are owned by the government and constitute a large part of the state-owned sector. The Indian government has only recently begun allowing private sector companies to instruments in which pension funds can invest. Some companies like LIC and UTI have significant stakes in Indian companies but are not activist shareholders. As a result in India there is no large institutional shareholder engaged in shareholder activism through its investments decisions like Calpers in the United States. Lastly, the time taken to deliver verdicts through the court system in India is inordinately long. This acts as a deterrent for minority shareholders to pursue legal action against companies.

In addition, lack of trained staff at the stock exchanges and SEBI to effectively scrutinize compliance, the high transactions costs in both primary and secondary equity markets making takeovers difficult, little competition among financial intermediaries and the state-run intermediaries and their significant amount of bad loans, which affect their ability to act as monitors have made the Indian corporate governance deficient.

Conclusion

Despite a long corporate history, the phrase "corporate governance" remained unknown until the late 1990s in India. It came to the fore due to a spate of corporate scandals that occurred after the first phase of economic liberalization. The above discussion has shown that ownership concentration, prevalence of insiders and principal promoters, lack of protection for minority shareholders, lack of strict enforcement rights of regulatory authorities, disregard for disclosure norms and transparency are some of the endemic features of Indian corporate governance regime. These features have restricted Indian corporate sector's progress on the path of good governance principles. Hence, it can be concluded that despite India's best efforts to adopt the best international CG practices, their implementation has remained inadequate due to reasons of path-dependency.

CG practices the world over have evolved over time and are still evolving in response to various corporate failures and systemic crises. The focus to date has been on the structural and process elements of governance. But to achieve truly effective corporate governance, companies need to view this issue as a strategic challenge instead of simply responding to recurring imposition of new requirements. The task of adapting, refining and adjusting corporate governance practices is an ongoing process. Corporate governance should therefore be considered as "work in progress" and its practices should be reviewed systematically and periodically.

5

Industrial Sickness: Some Solutions

Introduction

The liberalization policy initiated in 1991 was in part a response to the growing industrial sickness during the 1980s. During the early years of reform, the policy shift lived up to the expectations of policy-makers and the incidence of sickness registered a drastic decline, particularly in small-scale industry (SSI). However, this declining trend was reversed in 1997, when recession hit the economy. More than the SSI sector, the recession battered the large- and medium-scale industry (non-SSI sector). In the non-SSI sector, the average annual growth rate of sick units did not show any significant reduction in the 1990s. The real amount blocked in sick units with 100 per cent erosion of net worth showed only a marginal fall, proving that the economic burden of non-SSI sickness continued unabated. The government then prepared for a major overhaul of the rules and regulations regarding industrial sickness. The Sick Industries Companies Act of 1985 (SICA), which provided the legal framework for the rehabilitation/winding up of sick non-SSI units, is going to be repealed. The Board for Industrial and Financial Reconstruction (BIFR) – the body set up in 1987 to expedite the revival of sick units – has been would up, and the redefined burden of revival/winding up of sick units has been put on the national company law tribunal. In this context, it would be useful to look at the trends and patterns of sickness over the past decade and to compare it with those of the 1980s so as to examine whether the earlier strategies of the government have yielded results and whether the present policy reforms can be justified.

This paper is an attempt to trace the trends and patterns in sickness during the 1980s and 1990s with special reference to the large and medium sector. Further, sickness in the large and medium-scale sector is positioned against that in the small-scale sector. Studies conducted so far have not made any further revelations than that it is the non-SSI sector that constitutes more to the economic burden. However what is of greater concern is the extreme vulnerability of large and medium-scale units to external imbalances and sudden policy shifts. Section II deals with magnitude and growth of industrial sickness in India over the past two decades. Section III analyses the composition of sickness. The state-wise and industry-wise distribution of sickness is also studied. The performance of BIFR over the years is mentioned briefly in Section IV. Section V presents the summary and conclusions.

Magnitude and Growth of Sickness/Failure

Problems in the Data Set

Ascertaining the magnitude and growth of sickness in both pre- and post-reform periods is not an easy task. One major government source identified for obtaining data was the Economic Survey, which publishes data collected by RBI from commercial banks. However, the data was ridden with definitional and accounting problems, making comparisons almost impossible. For instance, till the end of 1988, the reference point was the end of December, which marks the end of a calendar year by shifting the reference period to the end of March, resulting in loss of data for one year, (1989), and thus affecting the continuity of the series. While studying non-SSI sickness, the data for 1990 can be taken as a proxy for 1989, though this value in the series refers of the level of sickness three months later. However, even this kind of approximation is not possible for SSI data due to the changes in the accounting of sickness. The data, for example, show a sudden upsurge in SSI sickness in 1982. This happened because the State Bank of India –the major provider of working capital to sick units-started including these SSI units in the protested bills/ recalled accounts in its list of sick units from that year onwards, making comparison with previous years impossible. Thus, one will have to avoid the use of data for 1980 and 1981. Again, in 1990 there is a sudden fall in sickness because of the exclusion of non-traceable and non-existent units from the sick SSI units list. Since the data on non-traceable and non-existent units were not given separately from 1990 onwards as well as for the period 1982-88, both pre-

and post-reform comparison of sickness for the small-scale sector was difficult to make. What can be done at the most is to take two periods in complete isolation and look for the trends within that period. The unreliability of on small-scale sector sickness makes the comparison of overall sickness for the two decades also liable to wide fluctuations. The trends and patterns in non-SSI sector sickness, on the other hand, show conformity and are amenable to comparisons. The data on non-SSI sickness is classified into "weak units" and "sick units", a defined by the SICA of 1985. The later will be called SICA units to avoid confusion.

The next issue to be tackled was the definitional problem. The periodic revision of definition of sickness was found less likely to affect the trend of sickness. There was a shift in the definition of sickness from complete "net worth erosion" to "repeated default on loan payment". The advantage of the latter definition is that sickness is detected at an earlier stage. From practical experience, on average, the year-wise distance between repeated default on loan payment and net worth erosion is not more than one or two years. In addition, the dual classification of non-SSI sickness – as sick and weak units – is supposed to take care of this issue. However, the discomfort of "weak" status must have forced firms to cover their sickness and go for creative accounting, where losses and net worth erosion appear only when it becomes impossible to hide the facts. This can be one reason why the percentage of weak units showed a decreasing trend over the years. For instance, 1980, 71 per cent of the total non-SSI sick units belonged to the 'weak" category. In 2002, the corresponding figure is 12 per cent. Given that failure has a history, this shows the extent of creative accounting by firms. This is substantiated by the fact that many of the annual reports do not show losses even when the firms are defaulters.

The definition of small industry (and hence of large and medium-scale industry) has also undergone a series of revisions except that of in real terms was insignificant for all revisions except that of 1997 (when the investment limit was raised to Rs 300 lakh from the earlier Rs 60 lakh), where the revised definition allowed for increased scope in investments. The government them lowered the investment criterion to Rs 100 lakh in 1999. When the investment criterion is raised in real terms, more firms will come under the purview of "small-scale industries". Hence, the number of sick units in the small-scale sector may also be large for that year. In other words, the number of non-SSI units may register a decline (and vice versa). However, such correlations are not visible in the trends presented by data. For instance, when the revision of definition entailed a decrease in the number of non-SSI sick units after 1997, the figures actually rose. This rise can thus be purely attributed to the recession that hit the economy.

As a result of these definitional and accounting problems attached to the Economic Survey data, different classification periods should be adopted for analyzing various aspects of sickness. The trends and patterns in sickness can be inferred from. In order to compare the degree of sickness for both sectors in both decades, an equal number of years before and after liberalization are taken. The pre-reform period is taken as 1982-88 and the post-reform period of 1996-2002 is considered, a classification that overcomes most of the problems associated with the data. The Economic Survey provides room for a comparison between SSI and non-SSI sector sickness and provides data for comparing sickness records in both pre- and post-reform periods. However, as mentioned above, the comparison of SSI sickness and hence the overall level of sickness in the two periods is still problematic. Other data sources used in the present study are the BIFR and the IDBI report on development banking, especially while analyzing the composition of sickness. A detailed account of non-SSI sickness is given in BIFR data given information not only about the number and accumulated losses of sick units, but also about their net worth and the number of workers displaced due to them. Since both IDBI and BIFR data sources do not trace sickness of the early 1982, while analyzing the composition of sickness, previous studies are taken as standards. All three sources exhibit a comfortable degree of conformity with each other in the trends and patterns portrayed.

The Indian experience with planning created an army of inefficient entrepreneurs and firms. The MRTP and import control regime created a set of high cost firms, which emerged as monopolies through a pre-emption of capacity, becoming highly diversified conglomerates with a lack of synergy in their operations and remaining as mini-projects without scale economies. The policy of reservation provided sufficient incentives for the firms to remain "small for ever" without bothering about scale and cost economies. The inherently underdeveloped, control ridden capital market ultimately led to the emergence of highly leveraged firms, which would be thrown out if protection was removed. Apart from there being many hurdles for entry, exit was also prohibited in order to protect labour interests, with a phobia towards closing even the most inefficient units. This made India the unique abode of industrial sickness, where firms that must otherwise have been thrown out of the market, continued to operate with government support. Thus, the average annual growth rate of sickness recorded by the Economic Survey was 40 per cent during 1982-88 in terms of number of units and 22 per cent in terms of the amount blocked in these units. This was mainly due to sheer size of sick SSIs – the most protected sector – which was growing at an unbelievable 42 per cent per annum. During this period, the policy aspect of sickness masks its other dimensions such as entrepreneurial incapability was considered to be a result of the specific policy regime, which failed to internalize the incentives. Thus, when small doses of liberalization were attempted as a part of the firefighting strategies, these firms were slattered, leading to their exit from the market.

The 1980s was, in fact, a decade of small industry sickness. The pre-reform period witnessed a massive shakeout in the SSI sector, which dominated the scenario with its high growth rate both in terms of number of units and amount blocked. Thus, the share of sick small units in the total amount blocked increased steadily from 17 per cent to 26 per cent by the end of the decade. However, the growth of sick units was arrested during the liberalization phase. The number of SSI sick units registered a negative growth rate from 42 per cent per year in the 1980s to –4 per cent per year in the 1990s. The real and nominal amount outstanding registered a drastic decline in the post-reform period. Thus, the share of sick SSI units in the total amount blocked declined to 19 per cent by 2002.

As mentioned earlier, a precise, overall comparison of sickness in the pre- and post-reform decade is difficult to make, owing to the definitional and accounting problems associated with the Economic Survey data on sickness in the small-scale sector. However, due to the wide gap in the two growth rates one can expect a declining rend in sickness in the small-scale sector, which is also reflected in the decreasing share of sick units in the total number of SSIs functioning in the country.

Nevertheless, the average annual growth rate in the number of non-SSI units falling sick remained almost constant at 5 per cent, both in 1982-88 and 1996-2002. But, the post-reform period – 1996-2002- has undeniably exhibited a declining trend compared with the pre-reform period, with reference to the real and nominal amount blocked in the non-SSI sector (including weak units). The nominal amount blocked in the non-SSI division during the two periods grew at 21 per cent and 12 per cent respectively. In real terms, it was 13 per cent and 8 per cent. Nevertheless, the economic burden of SICA units (whose net worth was completely eroded) continues, even though the rate of growth of such sick units has decreased drastically. The real amount outstanding in these units grew at 8.6 per cent and 7.4 per cent respectively during the pre- and post-reform period.

Also, a meager 1 per cent of sick non-SSI units account for around 75-80 per cent of the economic burden caused by all sick units in both decades, whereas the remaining 99 per cent of the sick units belonging to the SSI sector, account for, at the most, only one- fourth of the total amount blocked. The level of sickness in the non-SSI sector, defined as the percentage of sick units to total non-SSI units, showed an increasing trend, whereas the corresponding figures for the SSI sector exhibited a decreasing trend. The sick non-SSI units constituted around 2.4 per cent of the total number of non-SSI units both at end of 1988 and at the end of 1999. This means that the level of sickness has not come down in the non-SSI sector. On the other hand, the percentage of sick SSI units in the total number of working SSI units declined in the post-reform period. At the end of 1988, around 15 per cent of the SSI units were sick. This came down by to around 7.5 per cent in 1998, and rose to 10 per cent in 1999, when recession-induced sickness in the SSI sector began. SSI sickness seems to have stabilized during the post-liberalization period. It could be that their harvest was already done, particularly because their failure rate was around 42 per cent in the previous decade.

The gravity of the situation in the non-SSI sector can also be understood from the data produced by BIFR and IDBI. In contrast to the Economic Survey reports on sickness, the average annual growth rate of non-SSI sickness as per BIFR records (this corresponds to SICA units' growth rate in Economic Survey) is 18 per cent during 1991-2002. BIFR records detail the non-SSI sickness. As per BIFR records, till December 2002, 4,318 cases (all large and medium scale units) had been registered with it, since the broad's inception in 1987. Altogether, this accounted for an accumulated loss of Rs 89,050.67 crore. Of this 28 per cent was due to only 190 PSUs (4 per cent of the total). The sick units affected a staggering 22-lakh employees. The overstaffing of PSUs resulted in around 45 per cent of the employees being thrown out from the public sector alone, though these accounted for only 28 per cent of the accumulated loss and around 4 per cent of the total number of sick units. After 1992, PSUs halve not been referred to BIFR on a large-scale. The tremendous public criticism regarding the efficiency of PSUs towards the end of the 1980s must have led to some amount of streamlining, resulting in higher performance levels. In addition, there has been a change in government policy in favour of selling off PSUs to private entrepreneurs. Thus, the disinvestment spirit may also be responsible for the decline.

In both BIFR and IDBI data sources, as in the Economic Survey data, non-SSI sickness showed a sudden jump in 1997, with the onset of the recession. The Economic Survey shows that SSI sector sickness shot up only two years later, in 1999 and again declined. This time lag can be attributed to the flexibility and superior staying power of small industries in a depression phase. Many studies by SIDO and NCAER halve shown that technological advancement has made SSIs more efficient in the post-liberalization period, thus reducing their failure rate. In the recessionary years, their smallness itself is shown to be a blessing in disguise, especially when they are technically efficient.

Thus, while the SSI sector appeared relatively immune to the recession, the non-SSI sector fell easy pey to it. The later was heavily responsive to the problem years. This is reflected in non-SSI sector sickness trends, where a clear upward shift starts from 1987 in the pre-reform (the SICA units sickness jumps in 1986, soon after the introduction of policy reforms by the Rajiv Gandhi government and from 1997 in the post-reforms period, when the manufacturing sector growth rate declined by half (from 14.1 per cent in 1996 to 7.3 per cent in 1997). In 1997 itself, as per BIFR records, there was a 140 per cent increase in the incidence of sickness. In other words, the number of sick units increased by a factor of 1.4 from the previous year. Until then it was on a declining phase. In 1996, only 97 firms had been registered with BIFR. The next year the figure shot up to 233. The upward spiral reached its highest level in 2002, when the manufacturing sector registered a growth rage of just 2.7 per cent, with 559 firms registering with BIFR (However, IDBI and the Economic Survey are indicative of a recovery n 2002). From this we can infer that the recession/external factors and the incidence of sickness are showing a powerful correlation. It is time to concentrate on the factors that make our industries vulnerable to external factors.

Another factor of importance is the declining potential viability of these sick units. The data shows that in all the sectors the number of potentially viable units has been reduced to almost half over 10 years. The amount blocked on account of viable units has also shown a substantial reduction during this period. In the non-SSI sector, in 1990 the outstanding credit that could be redeemed was 44 per cent of total amount blocked in that division. In 2002, the amount that could be redeemed from potentially viable units is a mere 19 per cent. This is where the difference between the pre- and post-reform period lies. Now, once in the grip of sickness it is not easy for a firm to survive. Product and technological obsolescence can be one reason for the reduced viability of units. Also, in order to save face, the firms must have allowed sickness to grow by hiding it through creative accounting. Thus, even revised definitions to detect sickness at the incipient stage have not improved the viability of firms. Perhaps the revised definitions must have helped the financial institutions in retrieving some of the loan amount extended. Hence, winding up, rather than rehabilitation, appears as the best fire-fighting strategy in these cases.

Composition of Sickness

(a) Industry-Wise Distribution of Sick Units

An industry wise study showed that the composition of sickness has not changed much. Most of the sick units in the 1980s were from textiles, metals and chemicals sectors. Both IDBI and BIFR data are in general agreement regarding the top four industries on the sickness map. The shares of each industry as per the IDBI reports and BIFR records. The jute industry figured prominently in terms of its share of workers displaced, even though it accounted for very few sick units and accumulated losses. Similarly, BIFR records place the fertilizer industry in terms of accumulated losses, even though it accounts for less than 1 per cent of the total number of sick units. IDBI reports puts power projects as the main contender in the amount blocked. In the food products division, sugar and vanaspati and vegetable oils together accounted for around 70 per cent of the amount blocked and 50 per cent of the number of units. Similarly, drugs and pharmaceuticals constitute around one-third of the total sick units in the chemicals sector, proclaiming a crisis in the pharmaceuticals division marred by skewed patent regimes. A time series plot shows a sudden upsurge in 1997 in all these sectors. Besides 85 service sector units also appeared on the sickness map given by IDBI, in 1997.

Industries that figured prominently on the sickness map are those that received lesser assistance from financial institutions during the decade. Yet it cannot be stated emphatically that sickness in these industries was due to decreased flow of financial assistance, given that the composition if such has changed in pre- and post-reform periods. The causality can be the other way round. The dismal performance of these units must have forced FIs to reduce their assistance to them in the wake of increased efforts to cut down their NPAs. If the declining D/S ratio (amount disbursed/ amount sanctioned, which fell from 80 per cent in 1986 to 62 per cent in 2001) can be taken as an indicator of stricter scrutiny of investment proposals and an even stricter project follow-up, it can be said that the poor performance of these industries led to their lower share in the total assistance funds.

Table: Industry Share in Total Number of Sick Units and Amount Blocked 1994-2002

Industry	*Per Cent Share in Sick Units*	*Per Cent Share in No. of Amount Blocked*
Textiles	25.5	11.4
Metals	15.6	17.3
Chemicals and products	15.0	13.7

Food products	9.5	4.2
Electrical	7.3	3.4
Services	5.3	4.5
Paper	5.2	2.9
Transport equipments	5.0	2.8
Machinery	4.7	2.4
Cement	4.3	6.0
Electricity	2.1	18.2
Fertiliser	2.1	2.8

*Source:*3 IDBI Report on Development Ban in, various issues. E

(b) State-Wise Distribution of Sickness

In the 1980s, Maharashtra Gujarat and West Bengal figured prominently in terms of the number of sick units as well as amount blocked. However, the post-reform period points to the entry of Andhra Pradesh and Tamil Nadu into the top three of four positions in terms of the largest number of sick units. This is so in both BIFR and IDBI data for all the time periods mentioned. IDBI data also establish their predominance in the amount blocked. According to IDBI records, till 2001 Andhra Pradesh had the highest figure of amount outstanding in sick units in 2002 it was pushed to the second place. Tamil Nadu comes in fourth. However, BIFR records that cover the period 1987-2002 do not place these two states in any significant position with regard to the economic burden of sickness. The traditional seats of sickness – Maharashtra, Gujarat and West Bengal – figure high in BIFR data series, due to the wider time range. Also, the capital intensity of the project (which is reflected in the net worth of companies) that have gone bust in quite high for these states, resulting in their having a larger share of accumulated losses and workers displaced. Bihar, for instance, figures in the top-five list in terms of economic losses, though the number of units constitutes just 2 per cent of the total sick units. Region-wise and state-wise distribution of sickness and a comparative ranking of states as per the two data sets, if IDBI and BIFR. The growth rate of sick units over different time periods. The supremacy of the southern states in the IDBI data is due to the serve shakeout that took place in these states in association with recession, which is captured well in their time period – 1994-2002. For instance, if we look at BIFR data, among states with a significant share in the total number of sick units (Maharashtra, Andhra Pradesh, Tamil Nadu, Gujarat and Uttar Pradesh), Tamil Nadu registered an annual growth rate of 99 per cent during 1997-2002, when the national average was just 41 per cent. Andhra Pradesh occupies third position with 52 per cent. Similarly, when there was a 140 per cent increase in 1997 from that in the previous year, at the national level, the corresponding figure for AP and TN was 300 per cent and 480 per cent. This is greater than the most industrialized state of Maharashtra. Thus, southern states were the worst hit during the recent shakeout. When the national average of sickness was around 18 per cent, (for 1991-2002, as given by BIFR), the average annual growth rate of sickness for Tamil Nadu was 54 per cent. For AP, the corresponding figure was 20 per cent. This shows that southern states that embraced the new policy reforms in spirit and content were badly hit by the global recession.

Apart from this, BIFR data series provides a region-wise analysis on employment, net worth and accumulated losses of failed units. Just as industrialization was localized, sickness is also localized. In the northern region, UP and Delhi accounted for around 60-63 per cent of sick units and accumulated losses. Up alone has 46 per cent of workers displaced. The share of individual states in sickness represents an even higher concentration in other regions. For instance, in the southern region Tamil Nadu and Andhra Pradesh together accounted for 71 per cent of the total sick units and 74 per cent of accumulated losses. Andhra Pradesh alone has 35 per cent of the sick units and 36 per cent of the accumulated losses. Tamil Nadu contributes 36 per cent of sick units and 37 per cent of the accumulated losses in this region. However, 44 per cent of the workers displaced are from AP. IN the eastern region, West Bengal dominates with 65 per cent of sick units and unemployed workers and 57 per cent of losses. Next comes Bihar, which accounts for 16 per cent of units and 30 per cent of accumulated losses. This can be due to the greater presence of sick PSUs in Bihar. These two states, account for 83-86 per cent of the sickness in the eastern region. In the western region, Maharashtra leads, followed by Gujarat, with around 57 per cent and 26 per cent respectively in terms of the number of sick units. These two states together account for 83 per cent of the sick units and 86 per cent of the accumulated losses.

Though the southern states, mainly AP and TN, had made an entry into the sickness map in terms of the number of units, BIFR records show that their share in the economic loss is the least for the whole of India. Surprisingly, the eastern region, with the left-oriented, labour protective West Bengal has contributed to around 40 per cent of the workers displaced, in spite of having only 12 per cent the total number of sick units. This has happened because of the failure of big projects. This should be a matter of concern for the West Bengal government.

Performance of BIFR

BIFR was set up primarily to provide support to sick units through the speedy disposal of cases for winding up or rehabilitation. But BIFR's performance had come under heavy criticism almost since its inception. The Goswamy Committee, set up in 1993, criticized the preference of the board for rehabilitation rather than winding up, which resulted in undue delay without results. Even after the setting up of the debt recovery tribunals for the speeding up of the process, things have not improved at BIFR. Now steps have taken to wind up the organization. The year-wise performance of BIFR. Of the total 4,318 cases registered, hardly 9 per cent were revived by the end of December 2002. Another 24 per cent were dismissed as non-maintainable. The remaining cases are awaiting a decision. CMIE has pointed out that around 36 per cent of the cases were pending in 2001, and a mere 1.06 per cent could actually turn around. This gives credibility to the argument that BIFR only served to delay the liquidation process. In business circles the board came was made in budget 2001-02 to repeal SICA and amend the Companies Act in order to set up a national company law tribunal to which may be assigned the disputes now handled by Company Law Board, BIFR, AAIFR and the high court. The Companies Amendment Act 2003 came into effect on January e, based on the recommendations of the

Balakrishna Eradi committee, which was as set up to examine the law relating to insolvencies and winding up of companies. With this BIFR and its appellate authority, AAIFR, lost the rationale for their existence. Coupled with this comes the new ordinance, the Securitization and Reconstruction of Financial Assets and Enforcement of Security Interest Ordinance – promulgated in June 2002 (and regularized into an act in November 2002), which gives creditors the power takeover the assets/management of the defaulting company without the intervention of the court. These firefighting policies indicate a marked shift in the responsibility of industrial restructuring from secured creditors and financial institutions to the defaulting debtor firms.

Conclusion

In this paper, an attempt has been made to trace the trends and patterns in industrial sickness during the pre- and post-reform period, with focus on large and medium-scale units. In the 1980s, widespread inefficiencies in industrial establishments, sponsored by government policies, resulted in a steady increase in sickness. This was true in the small-scale sector – the most protected division of industry – during 1982-88, when around 15 per cent of the total SSI units were sick. During this period, SSI sickness was growing at 42 per cent per annum. The decade of the 1980s was thus a decade of SSI sickness. Coming to the 1990s, one can see that industrial sickness has been reduced. Though this cannot be stated emphatically owing to the definitional and accounting problems associated with data on SSI sickness, it holds true in the case of the non-SSI sector. The rate of growth of sickness has slowed down in the non-SSI sector. But this doesn't give us relief. After 1997, all industrial divisions and all states recorded an unprecedented continuing increase in sickness. Amidst claims that India would come out unscathed from recession, more and more firms are closing down. In 2002, there was a 21 per cent growth in the incidence of non-SSI sickness, as per BIFR records. In addition, a comparison of pre and post-reform non-SSI sickness shows that the economic burden of sick units whose net worth had eroded completely (SICA), did not show any remarkable reduction in the post-reform period. Compared with the SSI sector the reduction in the number of SICA units was not remarkable. Though the non-SSI sector forms only a meager 1 per cent of the total sick units, almost 75-80 per cent of the amount blocked by them. Also, 2.4 per cent of the total non-SSI units in the country were sick, both at the end of 1988 and at the end of the year 1999, when the corresponding figure indicated a reduction in the SSI sector. Thus, in general, the post-reform period is a period of large and medium-scale sickness.

The SSI sector sickness seems to have stabilized during the post-reform period, probably because it had already taken its toll. Also, while the non-SSI sickness showed a sudden jump in 1997 with the onset of recession, such a jump is visible in the SSI sector only after two years, that is in 1999. This can be an indicator of the greater resilient power of small firms compared with large firms. With technical efficiency in production, smallness can be an advantage during a period of fluctuations.

The industrial sickness of the 1990s catches our attention in many ways. Trends in the post-reform period sickness indicate the extent of creative accounting amount firms. This is reflected in the percentage of weak units, which registered a drastic decline. Not only that, the potential viability of sick units also declined. If 44 per cent of the total amount blocked could be retrieved from sick units in 1990, only 19 per cent of the amount can be retrieved at present. The decline in potential viability can also be attributed to fast-changing product preferences and technologies. However, this shows that even with continuous revisions in the definition of sickness, it was not possible to detect and repair sickness at the incipient state. BIFR, the body set up for just this purpose, turned out to be a colossal failure, with hardly 9 per cent of the cases referred it turning around. Even this is a doubtful figure. The poor performance of BIFR calls for its closure. The direction of the present policy reforms to shift the burden of corporate restructuring from creditors to defaulting firms needs to be appreciated, though one can differ in the minute details.

One matter of concern is the vulnerability of firms to external imbalances and sudden policy shifts. It needs to be explored why our industries fall easy prey to such developments. There is something that is common behind the sudden upsurge in sickness in 1986 and 1997 in the non-SSI sector. This means that we need to focus on the capital structure of our firms, which is believed to be the factor that makes a firm vulnerable to outside events. One other interesting factor is the emergence of the southern states-Andhra

Pradesh and Tamil Nadu-to prominent positions on the sickness map. The incidence of sickness in these states seems to be highly responsive to the onset of recession. It has to be kept in mind that these are the two states that embraced liberalization in spirit and content. So, it is of utmost importance to look at the factors that must have caused the sudden upsurge in sickness since 1997. One also needs to ascertain whether there has been any shift in the factors behind the sickness in the 1980s and 1990s.

6

Restructuring of SLPEs in India: A Microanalysis

Introduction

State level public enterprises (SLPEs) are an important component of the public enterprise system in India. According to the report submitted by the Study Group on Reforms on State Public Undertaking [Kurian et al 2002: vii-xiii] set up by the planning Commission in 2002, 747 SLPEs had a total investment of Rs 1,97,105 crore also on March 31, 1999. The investment in these enterprises as per the Institute of Public Enterprise (IPE) database increased to Rs 3,06,493 crore in 2002-03 [Mishra et al 2004]. The contribution of the SLPEs to GDP is about 5 per cent as compared to 10 per cent by the Central Public Enterprises (CPEs). The role of SLPEs and be assessed from the total turnover as a percentage of the gross state domestic product (GSDP). There was no consistent pattern among states and this percentage generally varied from 1 to 17 per cent of GSDP, with most states falling in the range of 6 to 15 per cent. Although SLPEs constitute 90 per cent of the total investment of CPEs, they are more than four times the number of CPEs. The average investment in an SLPE is 20 per cent of a CPE. However, the SLPEs in terms of resource use and control depict a different picture as compared to their counterparts in the central sector, in that they directly impact the functioning of the state economies and have a greater exposure to state political systems. SLPEs are characterized by weak middle management systems as they do not have on their rolls the requisite number of professionally qualified managers. The top management in these enterprises comprises mostly of an IAS chief executive officer and nominees of the state governments drawn from civil services, defeated politicians and the political party in power. The financial performance of the SLPEs bears the brunt of these shortcomings.

Between 1991-92 and 2002-03, SLPEs continued to incur net losses and showed the chronic tendency of accumulating losses. This macro analysis provides in the beginning an overview of the SLPEs in India, in terms of various financial parameters, followed by a discussion of the privatization scenario and the different practices of states in this regard. The differentiating features of privatization of SLPEs vis-avis CPEs have been outlined to highlight the challenges that various state governments have to meet in reconsidering the retention of their portfolio of SLPEs. The conclusion provides inputs to formulate an appropriate policy in this regard.

Financial Performance and Fiscal Impact of SLPEs

Typology

The sectoral distribution of the various SLPEs categorises these enterprises into manufacturing, financial, promotional, trade and service, utility and welfare sectors. In terms of the numerical distribution, manufacturing enterprises lead the tally, followed respectively by promotional, utility, welfare, financial and trading and services enterprises. Manufacturing enterprises dominated the scenario because the various state governments emulated the central government in giving a fillip to industrialisation. The trading and service enterprises received encouragement to provide an export thrust and create a suitable infrastructure of services at the state level. The promotional enterprises were set up to cast social activities with an economic tinge at the state level. The welfare enterprises were a new breed of SLPEs set up to provide economic support to the backward classes of society, comprising of scheduled castes, scheduled tribes, minorities, women and the handicapped. On the whole, Andhra Pradesh, Assam, Gujarat, Karnataka, Kerala, Maharashtra, Tamil Nadu, Uttar Pradesh and West Bengal showed a preference for manufacturing, promotional and financial enterprises. Maharashtra, Kerala and Uttar Pradesh set up a large number of welfare enterprises. The preference for economic and social choice. Andhra Pradesh, Delhi, Karnataka, Orissa, Tamil Nadu and West Bengal have a major share in the tally of utility sector enterprises. Utility enterprises comprise of state road transport corporations and the unbundled power sector enterprises.

Total Investment

The total investment comprises of the sum total of investments in the form of equity and debt capital by state governments and others, which includes the central government, holding company and financial institutions. The total investment in these enterprises for all the states taken together increased from Rs 77,730 crore in 1991 to Rs 3,06,493 crore in 2002-03. The lion's share, about 85 per cent of total investment belongs to utility enterprises. The major portion of total investment was shared by Andhra Pradesh, Delhi, Gujarat, Karnataka, Maharashtra, Punjab, Rajasthan, Tamil Nadu, Uttar Pradesh and West Bengal. The compound average growth rate (CARG) of total investments for the period 1990-91 to 2002-03 was 12.5 per cent. Investment grew at a slower pace during the period 1990-91 to 1996-97. The growth was much faster during the period 1977-98 to 2002-03. In 1997-98, the rate of growth of investment was high as it was the closing year of the Eighth Plan. In 1998-99, the rate of growth in investment maintained a high tempo as it was the opening year of the Ninth Plan.

Capital Employed

Capital employed comprises of the sum total of investments in the next fixed block and working capital. Net fixed assets indicate the investments in gross fixed assets minus accumulated depreciation. The investment in working capital represents the excess of current assets over current liabilities. Capital employed is also represented by the sum total of investment arising out of equity, long-term debts and internal resources. The investments by way of net fixed assets and working capital are financed by debt, equity and internal funds. The capital employed was Rs 73,300 crore in 1991. It increased to Rs 1,79,630 corer n 2002—3. The CAGR for capital employed was 6.74 per cent during the period under reference. The capital employed figure was about 50 per cent of the total investment, pointing to the fact that the SLPEs system was not organic and required artificial respiration from time to time. The states where this phenomenon had a forceful presence included Assam, Delhi, Goa, Gujarat, Haryana, Himachal Pradesh, Karnataka, Kerala, Maharashtra, Orissa, Punjab, Tamil Nadu, Uttar Pradesh and West Bengal, Rajasthan turned out to be an exception, indicating that viable and self-liquidating project management was the strength of the top management of SLPEs and policy-makers in the state government.

Net Worth

The net worth is derived by subtracting intangible assets, accumulated losses and fictitious assets from paid-up capital, and reserves and surpluses. The net worth was Rs 11,053 crore in 1991. It increased to Rs 44,631 crore in 2002-03. Net worth showed the trend to increase manifold; it turned out to be a shade lower than 7 per cent of total equity, which points to a negligible growth in net worth and the erosion of shareholders' basic capital in terms of real investment prices. The equity erosion occurred in Assam, Delhi, Goa, Kerala, Maharashtra, Mizoram, Meghalaya, Nagaland, Pondicherry, Sikkim, Tripura, Uttar Pradesh and West Bengal. These were precisely the states where the subsidies accounted for the major portion of losses incurred.

Total Revenue

This represents the top line of an enterprise, which provides a cushion against contingencies and the cover to meet expenses. Revenues should grow at least at a CAGR of 10 per cent to set off the loss caused by the real rate of inflation and meet the challenges of productivity arising out of technological advances and reorganization of business processes. The total revenue was Rs 36,112 crore in 1991. It increased to Rs 86,284 crore in 2002-03. This amount should be at least three times of the investment. The private sector multiple is five times. The multiple in the case of private sector enterprises abroad is eight times. The CAGR for total revenue for the period 1990-91 to 2002-03 was 6.93 per cent. Total revenue turned out to be a discouraging figure of about 40.6 per cent of investments in 1990-91 and 25 per cent in 2002-03. Total revenue comprises of the income from mainstream operations and others yields. The total revenue scenario speaks of many untold facts concerning the lack of marketing drive, quality consciousness and soft targeting. The states which earned more than average on a rupee of investment were only handful. In 2002-03, such states included Gujarat, Madhya Pradesh, and Tamil Nadu. All states in the country face the challenge of unlocking the vast untapped value in SLPEs.

Net Profits After Tax

Net profit after tax comprises of profits net of all expenses, interest and taxes. They determine the scope for and extent of allocations to reserves, dividends and surpluses. Net profit after tax is the "be all and end all" of business. It is not only the top line that is important for a business but it is also essential to ensure the bottom line is positive. Net profit after tax was Rs-938 crore in 1991. It fell to Rs-6, 997 crore in 2002-03. Net profit making helps in updating technology, it contributes to an organic growth and provides a unified direction. It adds to building up reserves and surpluses and higher earnings per share. Net profit making is the core element of corporatisation which takes place trough the concept of equity participation, limited liability, setting up strategic business units and practicing responsibility accounting. The operationalisation of these concepts create a harmonious internal environment where in different units/products groups and services compete with one another to improve their efficiency. Profitability strikes an optimum trade-off between demand side factors (revenues) and supply side factors (costs) in a competitive regime.

Net profits should at least be equivalent to the prime lending rate or 10 per cent of the revenues earned, which is the benchmark prescribed in financial management. Net profits for all the states taken together for the various years of the study, except 1994-95 and 1995-96, were negative. On an average, net losses, for all the states taken together, of the revenues earned were –2.7 per cent in 1990-91, which shot up to –8.0 per cent in 2002-03. Delhi, Gujarat, Haryana, Kerala, Maharashtra, Punjab, Uttar Pradesh and West Bengal have been major net loss makers during 2002-03. The net losses incurred by these states not only wiped out the total profits of profit making states but also were responsible for the phenomenon of loss making.

Accumulated Losses

The story of SLPEs is one of accumulating losses. The accumulated losses of SLPEs almost doubled from Rs 10,099 crore in 1991-92 to Rs 21,570 crore in 2002-03. The loss leaders comprise Andhra Pradesh, Arunachal Pradesh, Assam, Bihar, Delhi, Goa, Gujarat, Kerala, Jammu and Kashmir, Karnataka, Orissa, Pondichérry, Sikkim, Tamil Nadu, Uttar Pradesh and West Bengal. One of the reasons for the accumulated losses was an uncongenial debt equity ratio which was 4.27 for all the states taken together in 1990-91, decline gradually to 2.84:1 2000-03. This however resulted in no favourable consequence as most of the states had SLPEs incurring either cash losses of losses before interest and taxes.

Fiscal Impact on State Finances

The financial performance of SLPEs has a great bearing on the fiscal health of state governments. This impact could be explained in terms of two measures: Total impact on state finances (TISF) to states' own tax revenues (TRS) ratio and gross fiscal impact of state finances (GFISF) to states' own tax revenues (TRS) ratio. TISF could be shown in terms of annual outflows (sum of outflows resulting from change in state equity and debt and state subsidy and grants to SLPEs) plus the opportunity cost of investments in SLPEs. GFISF could be computed by adding the value of guarantees outstanding given by the state to the SLPEs during the year, to the value of TIST. GISF includes total; outflows due to the increase in state investments in SLPEs, state subsidies and loan waivers given during the year, imputed opportunity cost of state investments and additional guarantees extended to SLPEs during the year.

It is quite evident that finance of SLPEs substantially impacted state finances. TISF averaged over 31 per cent of states' own tax revenues, whereas the figure was nearly 120 per cent in the case of GFISF, with outstanding guarantees included. The outstanding guarantees have become a great threat to the financial soundness of the states for they are skyrocketing. They were in the order of Rs 1,01,343 crore in 2000-01. Subsidies and grants to these enterprises were about Rs 16,000 crore during the same year. The Ninth, Tenth and Eleventh Finance Commissions voiced their concern about the adverse impact on state finances due to the working of the SLPEs. However, the state governments have not been able to arrest the trend. Both the managerial and non-managerial factors retarded their financial performance. These varied from sub-optimal project management, deficiency capital budgeting and procurement systems to ineffective working capital management, unsuitable debt-equity ratio and absence of enterprise specific costing systems. The governing boards of these enterprises were packed by official nominees. As most of these enterprises are unlisted, they continue to escape from the application of Clause 49 of the Securities and Exchange Board of India Code on Corporate Governance, 2000 [SEBI 2000].

Privatisation Scenario

This section includes an analysis of the process of privatization, privatization policy, privatisation mechanisms, privatisation techniques, social safety nets, privatisation impediments and privatisation successes.

Process of Privatisation

The due diligence process for privatisation of the SLPEs is as follows:

Step 1: The government gives its approval for the privatisation/sale of an enterprise.

Step 2: The department of public enterprise (DPE) invites expressions of interest (EoI) through open advertisement for the selection of an advisor to assist in implementing the disinvestment decisions. Concurrently, valuation of the SLPE is undertaken in accordance with standard national and international practices.

Step 3: The Advisors are appointed, with the approval of the restructuring committee.

Step 4: Advisors assist the DPE in issue of advertisement for EoI from prospective buyers.

Step 5: The prospective buyers are shortlisted, using the prequalification criteria set out in the EoI advertisement.

Step 6: The information memorandum is prepared by the advisors, in consultation with the concerned SLPE; the memorandum is then given to the shortlisted prospective bidders, after they enter into a confidentiality agreement.

Step 7: The draft sale agreement and other legal agreements are prepared by the advisors and given to the shortlisted bidders to elicit their response.

Step 8: The prospective bidders undertake due diligence of the SLPE and hold discussions with the advisors, government, and management of the SLPE for any clarification.

Step 9: Based on the response received from the prospective bidders, the draft sale agreement and other legal agreements are fianalised, vetted by the law department, approved by the cabinet committee on disinvestment (CCD) and then sent to the prospective bidders for the invitation of final binding bids (Technical and Financial).

Step 10: After examination, analysis, evaluation and further negotiation, if necessary, the recommendations of the interdepartmental core group are placed before the CCD for the final decision regarding selection of the preferred bigger, signing of necessary legal agreements, and others ancillary issues.

It is clear that the privatisation process is very slow moving and cumbersome. The implementation mechanism is too complex at the central level. Some states governments have modified the mechanism adopted by the centre to their requirements, giving due consideration to factors such as transparency and speed. The cumbersome privatisation process adopted by the central government and various state governments in India has delayed the implementation of the privatisation programme and undermined the revenue potential from privatisation.

Privatisation Policy

As noted earlier, there has been a proliferation in the number of SLPEs and the investments their in have grown phenomenally. This has compelled state governments to have a relook at their SLPEs portfolio to decide which enterprises they wanted to retain and which ones they wanted to privatize, wind-up or restructure. While some states are open to both privatisation and/or restructuring, there are others such as Kerala, West Bengal, Tripura and Bihar which rejected the privatisation option and decided to go in for only restructuring/closure including reference to Board for Industrial and Financial Reconstruction (BIFR). Some states such as Madhya Pradesh, Karnataka and Kerala have announced detailed policies regarding the SLPEs portfolio. The government of Maharashtra in its industrial policy resolution announced the intention to private SLPEs.

Privatisation Mechanism

The state governments have preferred to set up expert committees to advise them about retention of the SLPEs portfolio. The government of Kerala appointed the Vijayachandran Committee and brought out a white paper on SLPEs in Kerala. The Institute of Public Enterprise undertook a study on behalf of the Asian Development Bank to recommend the portfolio for retention to the government of Madhya Pradesh. The S V Raghavan committee made specific recommendations for closure, privatization and restructuring of SLPEs in Tamil Nadu. Beside Kerala, which set up independent machinery to handle the restructuring of SLPEs, Punjab, Andhra Pradesh, Karnataka, Maharashtra, Orissa and UP also set up independent machinery on restructuring/privatization/disinvestment.

Privatisation Techniques

The state government adopted different techniques ranging from cold privatization (i e, non-privatisation reforms to transfer of ownership and closure of SLPEs). Kerala, West Bengal, and Tripura preferred cold privatization whereas Punjab, Haryana, Karnataka, Orissa and Andhra Pradesh opted for transfer of ownership through trade sale, divestment of majority stake and sale of equity by private placements. Tamil Nadu has preferred mergers and amalgamations.

Social Safety Net

Although the various states realized the significance of having a social safety net in the wake of privatization, they could not establish an adequate mechanism to deal with this issue chiefly because of the shortage of funds. However, Punjab was the first state to set up a state renewal fund on the pattern of the National Renewal Fund. Tamil Nadu, Maharashtra, Rajasthan, Karnataka, Madhya Pradesh, took their own initiatives in this regard. The National Renewal Fund did not extend any assistance to the states.

Privatisation Impediments

Privatisation and restructuring of SLPEs was fraught with a number of serious problems. Some state governments did not have a comprehensive understanding of the technicalities and accountability which formed an important part of the privatization process. The adjustment of the labour force through a voluntary retirement scheme (VRS) emerged as a complex issue. There were no arrangements put in place for a pre-investigation audit of all the activities concerning privatization/restructuring, in the absence of which a lot of witch-hunting took place. Political ideology also acted as an obstacle in the case of certain states. The location of states, in particular the north-eastern states, also obstructed privatization.

Privatisation Success

The political ideology and support the chief minister of states such as Andhra Pradesh, Karnataka, Punjab, Maharashtra and Kerala created a conducive climate for privatization. Public opinion was significantly molded by the opinion of the state chief ministers and policy-makers. The effectiveness of the machinery created for privatization lent further support to this phenomenon. The appeal of the enterprise and the readiness of the private sector, coupled with the negotiating skills displayed in the sale talks, also contributed to the success of privatization. Some states opened a dialogue with the employees of the enterprises that were on the privatization list and were able to weaken their resistance or draw their support. Another very important factor responsible for privatization was the preference of the private sector to buy/take over manufacturing enterprises. The size of SLPEs in terms of investment also weighed as an important consideration. These enterprises were mostly in the investment category of Rs 50- Rs 60 crore. Some states did not insist on full payment of privatization proceeds and allowed the buyers to pay in installments spread over two to four years. They also made the buyers agree to not effect immediate retrenchment.

Privatisation Practices

Andhra Pradesh

The Andhra Pradesh government appointed a committee to report on the restructuring of SLPEs.

Known as the Subramanyam Committee (1995), it had two non-official members. The commissioner of public enterprises was a member and convenor of the committee. The committee recommended nine SLPEs for closure, two enterprises for 100 per cent disinvestment, 10 enterprises for partial disinvestment and restructuring, two for restructuring and five for cost reduction and re-orientation. The committee's recommendations are under implementation.

A three-tier machinery consisting of the department of public enterprise, implementation secretariat and cabinet sub-committee on privatization, was evolved to effect disinvestments. As a part of economic restructuring in the first phase, the government focused on 12 small and medium SLPEs including some cooperative mills, whose restructuring and privatization did not involve complex institutional and social issues. The Adam Smith Institute (ASI) was appointed as the consultant.

The government also launched a safety net project for the redressal of social grievances. During the implementation of phase I, seven more SLPEs were added. In phase II, covering a period of five years between 2001 to 2005, 68 SLPEs were identified for privatization. It is however, interesting to note that Andhra Pradesh emerged as a leader in privatization in the mid-1980s by the sale of Allwyn Nissam and later Hyderabad Allwyn.

Kerala

Kerala had 111 SLPEs of which 63 were manufacturing enterprises. The SLPEs employed 53,270 personnel, An Enterprise Reforms Commission (ERC) was set up to have a relook at the portfolio of SLPEs and the recommendations of the Kerala Industrial Revitalisation Fund Board (KIRFB). KIRFB functions through the Restructuring and Internal Audit Board (RIAB). RIAB evolved a seven-fold categorization of SLPEs for restructuring and disinvestment. Group I enterprises with a negative net worth and obsolete product range were identified for closure. Group II enterprises with a negative net worth and incurring continuous losses due to operational reasons, were to undergo a comprehensive restructuring exercise to attract private investment. Group III enterprises with a positive net worth but incurring losses were proposed to be revived and made attractive for private investments. Group IV enterprises with a positive net worth and good record of profit earning were proposed to be further strengthened by private participation and accessing capital markets. Group V enterprises consisting of social enterprises were proposed to be retained in the state sector with budgetary support. Group VI enterprises comprising public utilities were proposed to be monitored by the ERC and retained in the state sector with the cost burdens to be passed on to the consumers. Group VII enterprises consisting of developmental and infrastructure agencies were to be examined on a case-by-case basis for their continuation in the state sector.

Maharashtra

The Maharashtra government constituted the Maharashtra Board for Restructuring State Enterprises (MBRSE) in August 2001. In January 2002, the state finance department identified 13 of the state government's 65 public sector units to be referred to the MBRSE. Of these, six have been referred to the board so far. These are Maharashtra Land Development Corporation (MLDC), Ahmednagar-based Chitale Distillery and Mafco, Haffkine Biopharmaceutical Corporation, Maharashtra State Road Transport Corporation (MSRTC), and Maharashtra Fisheries Development Corporation (MFDC). The board has recommended closure of MLDC, privatisation of Chitale Distillery and restructuring of MAFCO, MSRTC and MFDC. It has returned to the government its proposal to restructure HBC because any restructuring was to entail fresh infusion of capital and the Maharashtra's State Enterprises (Restructuring and Other Special Provision) Act, 2000, does not permit this. The board asked the state government to refer HBC to it once again for privatisation. Other SLPEs identified but not referred to the board included Meltorn, nine textile mills of Maharashtra State Textile Corporation (MSTC), Konkan, Vidarbha and Marathwada Development Corporations and Maharashtra Scooters, which falls under the Western Maharashtra Development Corporation (WMDC). In case of Maharashtra Scooters, the government is in talks with Bajaj Auto for the sale of 27 per cent of its stake in the company. Some other enterprises likely to be referred to the board included Maharashtra State Farming Corporation (MSFC), Goregaon Film City, and Kolhapur Film City.

Madhya Pradesh

Madhya Pradesh embarked on an Integrated Public Resource Management Programme (2001) under which integrated public enterprises reform was envisaged, with loan and technical assistance grant from the ADB. As part of the reforms, the government proposes to strengthen SLPEs in which government ownership is required to meet public purposes, close down those which are chronically sick and loss-making, restructure and divest the remaining enterprises to achieve greater efficiency, increase market discipline and have a wider dispersion of ownership. Accordingly, an empowered committee, headed by the chief secretary to the government and supported by a technical secretariat, was set up. It was also decided to transfer the responsibility of restructuring SLPEs from the administrative departments to the department of public enterprises, in order to accelerate the reform process.

Orissa

Orissa set up a cabinet sub-committee (1996) under former deputy chief minister which suggested closure and privatisation of certain units. Orissa availed financial assistance from the Department for International Development (DFID), UK for implementing the reform programme.

Punjab

Punjab set up a Disinvestment Commission in January 2001, which submitted its draft report in June 2002 that is now under consideration. The following principles were followed for recommending the restructuring, disinvestment and closure of SLPEs: *(a)* strategic and viable SLPEs be retained; *(b)* strategic but non-viable SLPEs be retained if their viability can be restored by necessary measures like outsourcing of activities; *(c)* non-strategic SLPEs be disinvested either by direct or strategic sale and SLPEs to be disinvested be freed from the administrative departments by allowing the implementation authority to take over their management; *(d)* the safety net of the employees of SLPEs be rationally chalked out through an adequate compensation package/retraining for deployment; *(e)* non-strategic SLPEs, which cannot be revived and in which no expression of interest by private parties is forthcoming, be liquidated and the management of the SLPEs be transferred to Punjab State Asset Management Authority for speedy disposal of assets. The Punjab State Asset Management Authority should be set up through legislation. The Commission recommended the following process for disinvestment.

(i) Each SLPE should be examined on its merits.

(ii) Management, labour and the general public should be given an opportunity of being heard.

(iii) Privatisation should not be confined only to loss-making units

(iv) VRS/retrenchment/compensation, cost of retraining, for redeployment, and retiring of long-term debts of SLPEs should be the first, second and third charge respectively on the sale proceeds from SLPEs to be disinvested.

(v) The proceeds from disinvestments should be placed in a disinvestment fund.

The government has set up a Directorate of Disinvestment to process the Disinvestment Commission's recommendations or come up with 'suo motu' reports in consultation with the commission. There is a three-tier structure to deal with disinvestments. There is a cabinet committee on disinvestments chaired by the chief minister. There is the core group of officer chaired by the chief secretary. The disinvestments directorate is the implementation agency. Punjab has put five SLPEs on fast track disinvestments. These included Punjab Tractors, Punjab Alkalis, Punjab Communications, Punjab Tourism Development Corporation and Electronics Systems Punjab. The advisors were appointed in case of six of these five SLPEs. A time frame of three to eight months was conceived to complete disinvestments in these enterprises. The Punjab government plans to use both the financial and strategic sale mode to privatize its SLPEs.

The draft report of the disinvestment commission has covered 29 SLPEs with their 11 subsidiaries and nine apex cooperative institutions. The state has provided total resources of Rs 8,430 crore out of which Rs 3,396 crore was equity investment in these enterprises as on March 31, 2001. The equity investment in 1987-88 was Rs 299 crore. The government received only Rs 8 crore as cumulative dividend till March 31, 2001, the total amount of outstanding guarantees was Rs 18.707 crore. The net loss incurred was Rs 185 crore in 2000-01. The accumulated losses were Rs 1,444 crore as on the same date. The SLPEs employed 1,18,624 personnel as on March 31, 2001, including the Punjab State Electricity Board.

Rajasthan

Rajasthan set up a committee on "Re-organisation, Strengthening and Disinvestment of SLPEs and Industrial Development". The government appointed an expert committee i e, the Mathura Das Mathur Committee on the restructuring SLPEs. The committee suggested privatisation of public enterprises which were low on both public purpose and profitability. A study of 11 SLPEs in Rajasthan suggests winding up of the Rajasthan Land Development Corporation, Rajasthan Cooperative Sheep and Wool Marketing Federation, Rajasthan State Agro Industries Corporation and Rajasthan Jal Vikas Nigam. It has suggested restructuring of Rajasthan State Hotels Corporation, Rajasthan Tourism Development Corporation, Rajasthan State Seeds Corporation, Rajasthan State Handloom Development Corporation and Rajasthan State Road Transport Corporation. As per another study, the enterprises recommended for priority closure are Rajasthan Electronics, Rajasthan State Granite and Marbles, Rajasthan Tungsten Development Corporation and Rajasthan State Agro Industries Corporation. The enterprises in the list of closure include Hitech Precision Glass and Rajasthan State Handloom Corporation. This study suggested mergers between Rajasthan Tourism Development Corporation and Rajasthan Hotels Corporation; Rajasthan Mineral Development Corporation and Rajasthan Minerals and Mines. As noted earlier, the departmental enterprises at Deedwana, Rajasthan Electronics and Rajasthan Land Development Corporation were lying closed/defunct for many years. The Rajasthan State Electricity Board is undergoing a reforms exercise as a part of which a State Regulatory Commission has been set up. Two SLPEs namely, Rajasthan State Tanneries, and Rajasthan State Salts prominently figured in the realm of privatisation.

Tamil Nadu

Tamil Nadu set up the S V S Raghavan Committee (1997) for streamlining and restructuring SLPEs and to initiate the privatisation process. The committee recommended setting up of a Tamil Nadu Public Sector

Disinvestment Commission. A three pronged approach was suggested for restructuring of the public sector retention, disinvestment and winding up. Tamil Nadu News Print and Papers, was privatised by reducing the government stake to 35.10 per cent.

West Bengal

West Bengal is contemplating closing down loss making SLPEs and welcomes private participation in state run enterprises. However, it intends to make the entire process a low key affair. A phased programme is being evolved wherein the long-term viability of all the SLPEs is being ascertained. The profit making SLPEs are to be retained, loss making SLPEs are to be retained, loss making SLPEs (large units) to be restructured and loss making SLPEs (small units) to be privatised. As of today, out of 89 SLPEs, 53 are manufacturing enterprises. Eight manufacturing SLPEs are profit making whereas 11 non-manufacturing SLPEs are profit making. The focus of the privatisation process would be on small sized loss making manufacturing SLPEs. The governments intends to turn around 14 manufacturing SLPEs through capital infusion, organsational and manpower restructuring and to divest them after turn around, keeping 24 per cent of the equity stake with itself. Prominent among these 18 enterprises are National Iron and Steel Company, Shalimar Works, Greater Calcutta Gas Supply, State Fisheries Development Corporation and West Bengal Mineral Development and Trading Corporation. At present, the state government is trying to build up a consensus to push through a minimum core programme. The restructuring exercise envisages carrying out optimization studies of the business of these 14 enterprises keeping in mind existing and foreseeable market demand trends. The entire exercise will be carried out in two parts. Part 1 will concern itself with evolving business optimization plans for four of these enterprises, identifying necessary business, financial and administrative measure for achieving long-term viability under government ownership. Part 2 will be devoted to identifying the earning potential of the remaining 10 enterprises and marketing the investment opportunities to secure investment of up to 74 per cent in their equity as joint venture entities.

PRIVATISATION IN SLPES: COMMONALITIES AND DISTINGUISHING FEATURES

This section discusses the commonalities and distinguishing features of SLPEs privatisation various states. It provides a comparative view of privatisation of the CPEs and SLPEs.

Commonalities

The following are the commonalities in the privatisation practices of the SLPEs in the various states:

(i) Most of the states explicitly or implicitly realized the need for the privatisation of the SLPEs. The fiscal crunch pressed them hard to go in for privatisation.

(ii) Many states formulated a public enterprise policy to consider afresh the retention of their SLPE portfolio.

(iii) Some states set up a mechanism to deal with the privatisation of SLPEs whereas many other were in the process of thinking about this issue.

(iv) Manufacturing SLPEs found a greater appeal for privatisation.

(v) A social safety net emerged as an important issue in privatisation exercise.

(vi) Trade sale was the preferred modality for the transfer of ownership.

Distinguishing the Features

The following were the main distinguishing features of the privatisation of SLPEs:

(i) Whereas states such as Andhra Pradesh, Karnataka, Punjab, Maharashtra, Orissa, Uttar Pradesh, Manipur and Assam showed a clear preference for privatisation, states like West Bengal, Kerala, Tamil Nadu, Madhya Pradesh and Meghalaya preferred restructuring.

(ii) Punjab, Maharashtra, Karnataka and Kerala set up the privatisation mechanism through independent enactments. Rajasthan, Haryana, Madhya Pradesh, Orissa, Andhra Pradesh, Assam and Tamil Nadu have either set up separate departments or used the existing mechanisms to handle issues related to privatisation.

(iii) Andhra Pradesh, Orissa, Kerala and Karnataka prepared phase-wise programme for privatisation of their SLPEs.

(iv) The privatisation programmes of Andhra Pradesh, Orissa and Uttar Pradesh received the support of DFID and were carried out with the support of foreign consultants. The Madhya Pradesh and Gujarat programmes received the support of ADB and were also carried out with the support of foreign consultants.

Centre Versus States

The following are the chief comparative features of privatisation relating to CPEs and SLPEs:

(i) The disinvestment/privatisation of CPEs began since the launching of the New Economic Policy in July 1991

(ii) whereas privatisation of SLPEs was resorted to much earlier in the case of the states e g, Allwyn Nissan, in Andhra Pradesh, UP Auto Tractors in Uttar Pradesh and Charge Chrome Plant in Orissa.

(iii) The states preferred trade sale as the modality of privatisation as compared to the partial disinvestment and strategic sale by the central government.

(iv) There was a trend in the states to prefer an independent legislation to execute privatisation programmes as compared to the executive action in the case of the central government.

(v) The privatisation exercise in state governments was not target-based whereas the central government laid down targets of the money to be mobilized through disinvestments/ privatisation.

(vi) The central government preferred to use the term "disinvestment" to ward off any ideological/political problem whereas state governments did not refrain from revealing their preference for privatisation. However, some states such as West Bengal, Kerala and Tripura rejected the use of terms viz, privatisation and disinvestment.

(vii) The privatisation of SLPEs, baring the State Electricity Boards (SEBs) turned out to be an easier exercise as compared to the CPEs because of their size and appeal.

(viii) The privatisation of both CPEs and SLPEs was confounded by the problem of transparency and valuation.

Lessons to be Learnt

The privatisation experiences of various state governments reveal the following lessons:

(i) It is easier to privatize smaller SLPEs.

(ii) Manufacturing SLPEs possess a greater appeal for privatisation.

(iii) Effective due diligence expedites privatisation.

(iv) The SLPEs organized under the Companies Act could be taken to market with greater ease and comfort as compared to the SLPEs orgainsed as public corporations.

(v) Valuation should be considered as an important element of the privatisation process. The entire valuation exercise should be made transparent.

(vi) In the case of loss making enterprises with multiple subsidiaries and product groups (strategic business units), restructuring should precede privatisation.

(vii) It is always helpful to establish a dialogue with employees before any action is initiated to privatize an enterprise.

(viii) Sole reliance should not be placed on any particular method of privatisation. Depending on the nature of the SLPE and market conditions, a combination of methods of divesting SLPEs should be employed to achieve the objectives of privatisation.

Conclusion

A dissection of the macroeconomic performance of SLPEs clearly reveals that their financial performance continues to cause a great deal of concern. According to the study group report on the reforms in state public sector undertaking for the period 1991 to 1998-99, instead of earning a 10 per cent rate of return, these enterprises registered a compound annual growth of 17.36 per cent in their net losses [Kurian et al 2002]. The fiscal impact of the viable working of SLPEs has become a cause of concern as the ratio of state finances to total revenue of states and that of gross fiscal impact to state finances have been found to be adverse. Policy-makers are left with no choice but to rethink the retention of the SLPEs portfolio in various states and to decide what to divest and what to retain. State governments overtly or covertly acknowledged the needed for privatisation of the non-core, continuously loss making and manufacturing SLPEs. The financial performance of SLPEs was such that it did not leave policymakers with much choice other than to redefine SLPE portfolios. Some states took the lead by putting in place a mechanism for privatisation and creating an environment conducive for the acceleration of the tempo of privatisation. However, there is no denying the fact that the states continue to face certain impediments in the successful implementation of their privatisation programmes.

It is apparent that both the select and the remaining states appreciated the need for disinvestment and privatisation an fiscal pressures mounted up and the need for accelerating social sector spending increased. Most states explicitly or implicitly realized the need or privatisation of the SLPEs. However, whereas states such as Andhra Pradesh, Karnataka, Punjab and Orissa showed a clear preference for privatisation, states like West Bengal, Tripura and Kerala showed their disenchantment with the term "privatisation" and opted to use the terms restructuring. The privatisation pattern of the central and state governments differed in many regards especially in relation to the method of sale. The central government referred partial disinvestment and strategic sale as compared to the trade sale modality popularly adopted by state governments. The privatisation experiences of state governments point to a number of lessons to be learnt for the future. Instead of depending on a specific modality, it would be beneficial to depend on a mix of methods.

7

Innovation Systems in India's IT Industry: An Empirical Investigation

Introduction

The software and services exports of India posted an impressive average yearly growth of 42 per cent from 1995-96 to 2004-05 and has been the envy of other hi-tech industries in India. The Indian software and services export sector in particular, which today employs more than a million software professionals, has zoomed from a mere US $ 12 million in the 1980s to a whopping US $ 17 billion in 2004-05. The software and services export segment (including ITES/BPO sector) has emerged as a significant export earner for the country contributing 34 per cent of total services exports and accounts to 64 per cent of the total information technology (IT) industry.

The Indian software industry has grown at a phenomenal rate over the second-half of the 1990s.

Earning around 80 per cent of its revenue from exports, the annual growth rate of software exports has between more than 45 per cent, except for then years 1999-2000, and the succeeding years from 2001-02 to 2004-05. The slowdown in export activity due to the worldwide recession and technological downturn has now abated, as the IT industry maintains its growth momentum and consolidates its partnership with overseas customers.

India's export-oriented software services industry not only recorded high growth rates but has also undergone some movement up the value chain, from code writing and software testing activities to systems integration, project management, high-end consulting, and packaged software exports. Effectively, India's software mix is a balance between on-site and offshore software services. It is said that the industry has perfected the global deliver model. The software and services sector is traditionally composed of customized software, largely driven by legacy applications and enhancement for existing systems, migrations to client-server systems and customs application development segment.

The ITES/BPO sector is the fastest growing segment within the software services sector. Within five years since its emergence in 1999-2000, its size grew to almost 10 times from US $ 565 million in 1999-2000 to US $ 5.2 billion in 2004-05. Within ITES services lines, customer care and finance have been the fastest growing segments. In terms of outsourcing of IT services, proficiency in the English language provides a comparative advantage of India's export vis-à-vis those of competitors such as China and Mexico. At present,

India's BPO has captured 44 per cent of total worldwide outsourcing.

Presently, India's software and services exports are oriented towards western countries, primarily the US. Around 62.7 per cent of India's IT services export revenues are realized from the north American market alone. In north America and western Europe, Indian software has been servicing significantly the banking, insurance, and financial services, manufacturing, communications and media, and government sectors.

A study by Nasscom and McKinsey on Indian IT strategies estimates that India can become important global player in IT and can reach exports between US $ 57-65 billion by 2008 – a manifold increase from US $4 billion in 1999-2000, from which IT services exports will take US$ 28.30 billion, ITES/BPO exports US $ 21-24 billion and product and technology services US $ 8-11 billion. Presently, Indian has evidently become a destination of choice not only for low-end work like ITES/BPO but also high-end development work like application design and implementation. More and more global companies are opting for offshore outsourcing combined with technological competence with lower cost, flexibility, quality and efficiency.

Indian companies have emerged as the most competitive suppliers of a large numbers of computer software in the world. The comparative advantages of Indian as a software exporter have been identified in its early growths years [Schware 1992; Heeks 1998 and 1996]; recent studies [Arora et al 1999; Kumar 2000a and 2000b; Krishna et al 2000; Arora and Suma 2001; Arora et al 2001; Kumar 2001a; Tschang 2001] have presented a wide range of critical factors that explain India's IT competitiveness. It success is now known to have resulted from a combination of abundant human resource endowments, linkages to the main export market, good timing, and the basic facilitation of infrastructure for communication and trading by the government. Moreover, government policies in building local technological capability and promoting enterprise level technological effort have met with success on a number fronts. These include building up one of the largest stock of scientific and technical manpower in the world. Indian talent has been widely sought by the IT industry worldwide.

Although India's success in the IT sector has been phenomenal and its software development is widely attributed to its human capital, it is not clear whether the growth has led to an industry-wide innovation. Parthasarathi and Joseph (2001) argued that the innovative behaviuor of firms under export orientation has been one wherein firms have depended heavily on collaboration with their foreign counterparts. Foreign firms, which possess the property rights for new technologies, usually assign specific tasks to Indian firms that do not require any serious research and development (R&D) efforts. Thus, R&D intensity in the industry has been negligible and has not recorded any market increase. On the other hand, Hagel and Brown (2001) found that Indian companies have also been able to export technology-intensive goods as well as technology itself to a number of countries. However, with the increasing need for many firms in the developed countries to outsource their IT operation, most of India's IT industry appears to have followed the path of export services father than develop its own brand products. In fact, from the R&D point of view, the nature of the IT industry was found to be applies", "service-oriented", or "incremental" in its innovation [Tschang et al 2003].

Recent studies about innovation in the industry however point the study of factors underlying innovation that go beyond skills, organizations, and in-house R&D to include knowledge spillovers, the broader innovation system, and linkages within a system of innovation. In the case of the hi-tech knowledge intensive sector, innovation is the key to competitive success, knowledge is a key asset and learning is a key process. Innovation as a key factor in competitiveness is particularly important in knowledge-based economy since hi-tech firms may more readily exchange tacit creative knowledge with each other and with university research laboraties and public or private research institutes as well as with the local or regional innovation support infrastructure [Smith 1997].

Kumar (2001a) specified the elements of India's systems of innovation to include government polices to create infrastructure for development of human resource, institutional framework and infrastructure for technological development, government's direct participation in scientific and technological development, incentive promotion of in-house R&D activity in industry, enactment of the new Patent Act, and encouragement to utilization of indigenous technology. He argued that the substantial investments made by the government in building the national system of innovation (NSI) over the past 50 years helped in improving the overall competitiveness of the industry. In a later study, Kumar and Joseph (2004) pointed out that the NSI which evolved as an outcome of government policies, has been instrumental in facilitating India's IT success.

Furthermore, Kaul (2002) in his study on innovative clusters and implications for public policy argues that new types of policies are needed to address systemic failures, particularly policies directed to networking and improving "firm absorptive capacities". Enhancing the absorptive capacities of firms is another policy priority. Technology policies should aim not only on technology-based firms but also at firms with lesser technological capabilities in traditional and mature industries, and in services sectors.

In spite of the build-up of these elements of the innovation system, there is some evidence leading to a systemic failure, which impedes the innovation performance of the IT industry. The lack of interaction between the actors in the system, mismatches between basic research in the public sector and more applied research in industry, malfunctioning of technology transfer institutions, and information and absorptive deficiencies on the part of the enterprises, all contributed to the poor innovative performance of the IT industry. Therefore, there is a need to direct the attention of policy-makers to this systemic failure to address the specific issues and apply the necessary remedy.

The paper is an exploratory study focusing on the strategies of firms in the Indian IT industry and their innovative behaviour from the point of view of the innovation system. The specific question that this paper attempts to address is: what type of innovation system exists in the Indian IT sector? In other words, the paper will determine the elements which define Indian

IT industry. Therefore, there is a need to direct the attention of policy-makers to this systemic failure to address the specific issues and apply the necessary remedy.

The rest of the paper is organized in the following manner. The section that follows examines the different elements of the system of innovation existing in the Indian IT industry in general. The third section presents the results of the survey examining the internal functioning and innovation of respondent-firms, their innovation and cooperation with other firms, academe, and technology support institutions, and the diffusion of knowledge and technology within the firms. And finally, the fourth section concludes the study by integrating the research output and the major findings of the survey. An attempt is made to identify the gaps in policy-making and implementation to improve the IT industry's system of innovation.

Innovation System in India's IT Industry

Gaining and sustaining competitive advantage in knowledge-intensive industry like IT means that enterprises need to focus on dynamic improvements and innovation. Innovation is fundamentally a learning process. Such learning – by "doing", by "using", by observing from, and sharing with others – depends upon the accumulation and development of relevant knowledge of a very wide variety. The recent literature on innovation systems [Nelson 1993; Lundvall 1992] stresses the fact that national specificity of patterns of interaction between users and producers of innovations are at the very core of what defines a national innovation system. More recently, there has been a growing interest in innovation systems at the regional level. At this level, clustering of innovative firms, their emergence, and promotion are becoming the focus of study. The innovation system can also be defined and studied at the sectoral level. A sectoral system of innovation and production encompasses new and established products for specific uses and the set of agents carrying out market and non-market interactions for the creation, production, and sale of their products [Malerba 2002].

The sectoral system of innovation in the IT sector of India can be characterized by the early development of a system of higher education in engineering and technical disciplines; creation of an institutional infrastructure for science and technology (S&T) policy-making and implementation; building centers of excellence; investments in public-funded R&D institutes and support for their projects, which crowds in private sector investments; and a unique social-cultural environment that supports the sustainability of these elements of the innovation system.

Since the early 1960s, the government of India has recognized the critical importance of the electronic and computing industries for national development. In view of their pervasive applications, the government has consciously strived to build local institutional infrastructure for development of local capabilities. These early initiatives have provided a base for the rapid development of the IT industry in the 1980s and 1990s.

The Indian strategy of the 1970s until mid-1980s was aimed at autonomous, national and state-led development of the computer and software industries.

Planning was used to direct investment to particular sectors. Expenditure on R&D, high tariffs on imports, limitations on foreign direct investment, the licensing of production capacity, and legislated monopolies for certain public enterprises were all examples of intervention designed to pursue specific national objectives in the IT sector. It was in this policy thrust that publicly owned and managed companies like Electronics Corporation of India (ECIL), Electronics Trade and Technology Development Corporation (ETTDC), Bharat Electronics (BEL) and Computer Maintenance Corporation (CMC) were created.

The computer policy of 1984, for the first time, acknowledged the importance of software development and underlined the needs for institutional and policy support. Policy shift towards the market mechanism began in 1986 that gradually reduced government control and a larger role was given to Indian private corporations. Accordingly, an explicit software policy was announced underlining the importance of an integrated development of software for the domestic and export markets giving more incentives for the industry to grow, such as tax holidays, tax exemption on income from software exports, export subsidies, and duty-free import of hardware and software.

With economic reforms beginning 1991, a number of other policy initiatives have facilitated the growth of IT. The new policy included the provision to finance software development through equity and venture capital, measures to make available faster and cheaper data communication facilities, removal of entry barriers for foreign companies and reduction and rationalization of taxes, duties and tariffs [Narayana Murthy 2000].

Likewise, the central government intensified its support for research and development activities, giving rise to institutions such as Centre for Development of Advanced Computing (C-DAC) and Electronics Research and Development Corporation (ERDC). But it was the creation of a series of software technology parks under the aegis of the Software Technology Park of India (STPI) that soon revolutionized the development of the software industry. Which led to the mushrooming of several local IT companies. As of now thee are 18 software technology parks in the country and they play a significant role in the software export.

Humanpower development particularly in the field of S&T has been India's core policy since 1985. As a result, a large number of institutions training S and T personnel were set up in the country. Premier institutions such as the six Indian Institute of Technology (IIT) and the Indian Institute of Science (IISc) which institutionalized engineering education in the country, led to the introduction of computer science degrees both in the undergraduate and graduate levels. Soon after, several local engineering colleges emerged owing to the demand of highly skilled humanpower in the IT industry. To this, government has quickly responded by facilitating the entry of the private sector in the training of software personnel by putting up an accreditation scheme based on certain objective criteria. As a result, a large number of private organizations were set up that provides short term training programmes catering to the middle- and lower-level manpower requirements of the IT industry. To a certain extent the National Centre for Software Technology (NCST) – a government agency that was created primarily to undertaken R&D activities related to computer technology and software design–contributes as well to the supply of skilled humanpower requirements via its short-term courses. Besides these, seven Indian Institutes of Information Technology (IIT) were set up to train humanpower on par with the academic standards of the IITs, coupled with strong support from the industry.

Since the early 1970s, the Department of Electronics (DoE), now transformed to the Ministry of Information Technology (MIT), has put heavy emphasis on R&D activity relating to the development of computer software by supplying R&D activity being done by different institutions such as Tata Institute of Fundamental Research (TIFR), IITs, IISc, ERDC and the Council of Scientific and Industrial Research (CSIR). These centers of excellence have been proven is instrumental for the development of technology in computer, electronic, and software and have even provided high-end expertise and manpower for the IT industry. The government has also stimulated and supported the R&D activity of industry through tax incentives and direct funding on a limited scale. A large number of academic institutions, industries and research labs with geographical distribution spread all over the country have implemented projects and programmes supported by the MIT.

Other support institutions also played a very important role in the sectoral system of innovation. For one, venture capital companies that became operational in India since the 1990s provided greater access to capital and encouraged professional business practices from their beneficiaries. Both the public and private sectors have developed venture capital funds for the software and IT companies, giving rise to software exports coming from several start-up software companies. Moreover, the software movement gathered momentum ever since the National Association of Software and Services Companies (Nasscom) came into existence in 1988. Presently, with more than 860 IT software and services member companies constituting almost 95 per cent of the revenue of the software industry in India, Nasscom has earned its place as India's apex body and umbrella organization, which assiduously promoters and catalyses the growth of all IT companies in and outside India.

Besides institutions and other support infrastructures, some socio-cultural factors have contributed to the Indian IT success. It is argued that the management practices and organizational modes that have emerged in the software industry are in convergence with the Indian socio-cultural ethos. Factors like value for intellectual activity, affinity and strength for maths and sciences, view of work as duty to family, and open communication across level in corporate and strategic decision-making that stimulate new ideas, have attracted a large number of young workers to the software industry.

Despite the early structuring of the system of innovation, it seems however that the software industry has not benefited much from it in terms of its innovative behaviour. The Indian software industry has revealed little thrust on R&D so far compared to the knowledge intensity and its international orientation. Government support for R&D in the IT sector increased only marginally from Rs 316 crore in 1994-95 to Rs 318 crore in 1999-2000 [Chandrasekhar and Basvarajappa 2001]. The IT sector is ranked third with respect to value addition, but is ranked eight in terms of R&D support. Innovation activities have remained largely Internal, especially among the large corporate firms. Though R&D spending by companies increased from Rs 97 crore (US $32 million) in 1994-95 to Rs 203 crore (US $45 million) in 1999-2000, their R&D expenditure has been rather low compared to international standards.

A bigger R&D thrust will be necessary for the Indian software enterprises to upgrade their export profile to higher value adding services and products, and establish themselves as innovators and developers of new products and technologies rather than just providers of coding and programming services [Kumar 2001b]. Experts also believe that in terms of implementing R&D projects between the IT sector and other areas like space technology, while coordination takes place on a need basis, organizations involved projects as well as policy continue to function largely as islands with very little networking [Chandrasekhar and Basvarajappa 2001].

Results of the Survey

With the aim to examine and understand the innovative behavior of Indian IT sector using the concept of a sectoral innovation system, a survey was conducted. A cluster sampling methodology was used to identify companies located in Delhi, Mumbai, and Bangalore. These three locations have the highest concentration of IT companies accounting for 60 per cent of IT companies as per Nasscom's survey. Within these clusters, we selected 300 companies from Nasscom's list of member-companies available in their website. A questionnaire was developed to collect information from these companies.

A letter was sent to all the selected companies along with a copy of the questionnaire by post. At the second stage, al the selected companies were called by phone and requested to participate in the study. A personal visit to Mumbai and Bangalore was undertaken to follow-up. However, in spite of the intensive and extensive efforts to get the questionnaires filled up by the prospective respondent firms, only 35 companies have responded affirmatively.

A large majority of the respondents belong to the software services sector as their primary activity, even though some of them, to some extent, are into software product manufacturing. From among them, only one is exclusively into hardware manufacturing, one a BPO company and one into training and education. Apart from being service-oriented, the sampled firms are predominantly export-oriented. On the basis of size, 18 per cent of the total are small units, 35 per cent are medium-sized firms and 47 per cent are large firms, which also follows the pattern distribution according to the age of firms. Most of the respondents were Indian companies, 17 per cent of which were 100 per cent foreign-owned.

Responses collected from these companies have been analysed. To get a further insight into the innovative behaviour of IT companies, an in-depth study of three companies was undertaken. The results of all these analyses are given below.

Innovation Behaviour of IT Firms

As far as the innovation behaviour of IT firms is concerned, shows that a larger proportion of the respondent firms are aiming at incremental innovations. Ninety-four per cent of them have improved, from a technological point of view, their productive processes. Not far behind, 89 per cent of them have improved their existing product and/or service.

With respect to radical innovations, 80 per cent claim that they have introduced new productive processes and a little less than three-quarter of the respondents have introduced into the market new or technologically innovative products and/or services. These figures may be an overestimation from what they really are. The fact is that since firms in the software and services sector are engaged into customized application development and maintenance, it requires principally an adoption of a particular leading edge technology as per the client's specification rather than the creation of an entirely new technology.

Nevertheless, on the basis of these results, it is still evident that IT firms are more inclined towards the improvement of their existing products, services or processes rather than introducing entirely new products, services or processes rather than introducing entirely new products, services or processes.

ISO 9000, benchmarking, flat hierarchies, and networking are among he most widely used organizational innovations by the IT firms in India. These organizational practices are inextricably linked o the firms' objective to produce high quality products or services within the required period of time.

Internal Functioning and Innovation

The pressures of globalization and the heightening of competition have forced firms to become more innovative. Because of competitive factors like the rapid changes in technology and at the same time an increasing demand for better quality at reasonable costs from sophisticated

Table: Type of Innovation in IT Firms

Type of Innovation	*Number*	*Per Cent*
Incremental		
Improved product/service	31	89
Improved productive process	33	94
Radical		
Introduced new product/service	26	74
Introduced new productive process	28	80

markets, companies have to choose from very limited strategic choices.

In This Study These Factors Were Classified Into Four Groups

(1) competitive challenges perceived by the company; *(2)* corporate response to the perceived challenges; *(3)* factors contributing to competitive edge; and *(4)* factors sustaining competitive edge. The specific factors were identified for the respondent firms to rate them on scale of 0 to 7. Unanswered items were given the value of 0. Using the ratings, the number of respondents was determined under three divisions: *(a)* those who rated the variable below 4 (that is the midpoint from a scale of 0 to 7); *(b)* those who rated the variable exactly at 4; and *(c)* those who rated the variable more than 4.

Most of the companies have perceived a very fast rate of change of technology in the industry, very frequent introduction of new products, very intense promotion, advertising, and selling, very intense competition in quality and variety of products or services, as well as price. Also, there is a fairly high degree of difficulty in hiring skilled personnel as well as their increasing remuneration. On the other hand, most of them do not find difficulty in obtaining supplies. Moreover, results show that there is genuine difficulty in obtaining finance from venture funds, consumer demand is almost predictable, and government policy for human resource availability, taxation, promoting R&D and the like are generally favourable.

In terms of corporate response to these perceived competitive challenges. A fairly high number of the respondents resort to cost cutting, organization restructuring, increasing speed of product development, intensifying internal R&D, intensifying marketing cooperation, increasing market share in their existing product-mix or market, and developing internally a new product and service in response to rapid technological changes and increasing market competition in the global IT industry. On an average, some have resorted to subcontracting and outsourcing as a way to cut cost and also ventured into technological cooperation to be abreast in the latest technologies and to penetrate new markets. Acquiring other businesses and having joint ventures with other firms are less adhered to as a response to the perceived challenges.

From the standpoint of the factors that contribute and sustain the firm's competitive advantage, perception as to the relative importance of the factors specified. A large majority of the respondents rated very highly customer-oriented factors: personal attention to customer needs, product/service quality or design, after sales service or maintenance, ability to quickly adapt to clients needs, quick and timely delivery, and price of products and services. For some of the respondents, regularly introducing new and unique product or service is another way to achieve customer satisfaction. Surprisingly, technology-oriented factors such as copyright or patent of new products, regular modernizing and replacement of capital equipment and regular purchase of the latest technology do not seem to be as important as the factors directly related to the customer.

As to the factors that sustain competitive advantage, skilled and capable employees, specialized expertise or products, top management, and improving continuously operational efficiency and financial strength of the company are perceived by most firms as the most important ones. Also to a certain extent, the range and variety of expertise or products, continuous resources allocation for R&D capabilities, geographic proximity to customers, information system and networking, capability of entering and managing technological alliances, reward system and compensation package, capability of combining different technologies, and established a marketing channel for distribution are important factors. Respondents are neutral in taking aggressive promotion sustaining competitive advantage. On the other hand, geographic proximity to suppliers and use of joint ventures for R&D are seen as less important factors to sustain competitive advantage.

Bibliography

Balakrishnan, P., K. Pushpangadan (1998): 'What Do We Know about the Productivity Growth in Indian Industry?' *Economic and Political Weekly,* August, pp 2241-46.

Balakrishnan, P., K. Pushpangadan and M. Suresh Babu (2002): 'Trade Liberalisation, Market Poser and Scale Efficiency in Indian Industry', Centre for Development Studies, Working Paper Series, No 336, Thiruvananthapuram.

Baldwin, R. John (1998): *The Dynamics of Industrial Competition, a North American Perspective,* Cambridge University Press, UK.

Basu, K. (1993): *Lectures in Industrial Organisation Theory,* Blakewell Publishers, Oxford, UK.

Boyle, SE and RL Sorenson (1971): 'Concentration and Mobility: Alternative Measures of Industrial Structure', *Journal of Industrial Economics,* XIX No. 2, April, pp. 118-32.

CMIE (1997): *Prowess Users' Manual,* Vol. 1, Mumbai.

– (2001), Prowess (Electornic Data), Mumbai.

Collins, N.R. and L.E. Preston (1961): 'The Size Structure of the Largest Industrial Firms 1909-1958', *American Economic Review* 51, December, pp986-1011.

Curry, B. and K.D. George (1983): 'Industrial Concentration: A Survey', *Journal of Industrial Economics,* Vol. XXI, No. 3, pp. 203-55.

Goldar, Bishwanath (2004): 'Indian Manufacturing: Productivity Trends in Pre- and Post-Reform Periods', *Economic and Political Weekly,* November, pp5033-43.

Gort, M (1963): 'Analysis of Stability and Change in Market Share', *Journal of Political Economy,* 71, February, pp 51-63.

Hart, P E, and S Prais (1956): 'The Analysis of Business Concentration', *Journal of the Royal Statistical Society,* CXIX, Pt 2, A119, pp150-81.

Hymer, S. and P. Pashigian (1962): 'Turnover of Firms as a Measures of Market Behaviour', *Review of Economics and Statistics,* Vol. XLIV, pp. 82-87.

Ijiri, Y. and H.A. Simion (1977): *Skewed Distributions and the Size of Business Firms,* North Holland Publishing Co, Amsterdam.

Joskow, J. (1960): 'Structural Indicia: Rank-Shift Analysis As a Supplement to Concentration Ratios', *Review of Economics and Statistics,* Vol. XLIV, pp. 82-87.

Krishna, K.L. (2004): 'What Do We know about Sources of Economic Growth in India?' National seminar on Planning and Development: Institutions and Markets, Dept. of Economics, St Thomas College, Thrissur, Kerala.

Pushpangadan, K. and N. Shanta (2005): 'An Order

Preserving Turnover Index and Market Behaviour', Centre for Development Studies, Thiruvanathapuram, mimeo.

Scherer, F. M. (1979): *Industrial Market Structure and Economic Performance,* Rand McNally and Co, Chicago.

Shalit, S and U Sankar (1977): 'The Measurement of Firm Size', *Review of Economics and Statistics,* Vol LIX, No. 3, pp. 290-98.

Shepherd, W.G. (1975): *The Treatment of Market Power: Antitrust, Regulation, Public Enterprise,* Columbia University Press, New York.

Simon, H A and C P Bonini (1958): 'The Size Distribution of Business Firms', *American Economic Review,* XLVIII, pp. 607-17.

Singh, A. and G. Whittington (1968): *Growth, Profitability and Valuation,* Cambridge University Press, London.

Suresh M. Babu (2002): "Economic Reforms and Entry Barriers in Indian Manufacturing', Centre for Development Studies, Working Paper series, No 331, Thiruvananthapuram.

Sutton, J. (1997): 'Gibrat's Legacy', *Journal of Economic Literature,* Vol. XXXV, pp40-59.

Abowd, John M. (1990): 'Does Performance-Based Managerial Compensation Affect Corporate Performance?', *Industrial and Labour Relations Review,* 43 (3), pp52-73.

Baker, George P., Micheal C. Jensen and Kevin J. Murphy (1988): 'Compensation and Incentives: Practice vs Theory', *Journal of Finance,* 43 (3), pp593-617.

Bebkchuk, L.A and F.M. Fried (2003): 'Executive

Compensation as an Agency Problem', NEBR Working Paper No 9813, National Bureau of Economic Research, Cambridge, Massachusetts.

Bhattacharya, Asish K and Sadhalaxmi V Roa (2005): 'Agency Costs and Foreign Institutional investors in India', Working paper No 548, IIM Calcutta, Kolkata.

Bhattacherjee, Debashish, S Jairam and G Ravi Shankar (1998): 'Top management Remuneration and Firm Performance: An Exploratory Analysis', *Economic and Political Weekly,* Review of Management and Industry, 33, pp10-15.

Core, John E, Robert W Holthausen and David F Larcker (199): 'Corporate Governance, Chief Executive Officer Compensation, and Firm Performance', *Journal of Financial Economics,* 51(3), pp371-406.

Davila, Antonio and Fernando Penalva (2004): 'Corporate Governance and the Weighting of Performance Measures in CEO Compensation', Working Paper No. 556, IESE Business School, University of Navarra.

Finkelstein, S and R A D' Aveni (1994): 'CEO Duality as Double-Edged Sword: How Boards of Directors Balance Entrenchment Avoidance and Unity of Command', *Academy Journal of Management,* 37(5), pp. 1079-1108.

Ghosh, Arijit (2003): 'Board Structure, Executive Compensation and Firm Performance in Emerging Economies: Evidence from India', IGIDR Working Paper Series, IGIDR, Mumbai.

Jensen, Michael C and William H Meckling (1976): 'Theory of the Firm: Managerial Behaviour,

Agency Costs and Capital Structure', *Journal of Financial Economics,* 3(4), pp. 225-64.

Jensen, Michael C and Kevin J Murphy (1990a): 'CEO Incentives: It's Not How', Harvard Business Review, 68 (3), pp 138-54. – (1990b): 'Performance Pay and Top Management Incentives', *Journal of Political Economy,* 98 (4), pp. 225-64.

Khanna, Tarun and Krishna Palepu (1997): 'Why Focused Strategies May be Wrong for Emerging Markets', *Harvard Business Review,* 75(4), pp. 41-51.

Milgrom, P and J Roberts (1992): Economics, Organization and Management, Prentice-Hall.

Murphy, Kevin J (1986): 'Top Executives Are Worth Every Nickel They Get', *Harvard Business Review,* 64 (2), pp125-32.

Pukthuanthong, Kuntara, Eli Talmor and James S. Walace (2004): 'Corporate Governance and Theories of Executive Pay', *Corporate Ownership and Control,* 1(2), pp94-105.

Ramaswamy, K., R. Veliyath and L. Gomes (200): 'A Study of the Determinants of CEO Compensation in India', Management International Review, 40(2), pp167-91.

Rui, Oliver M., Micheal Firth and Peter M. Y. Fung (2002): 'Corporate Governance and CEO Compensation in China', abstract = 337841, last accessed on January 14, 2006.

SEBI: Issues under clause 49 and proposed amendments, last accessed on December 25, 2005.

Swami, P (2005): 'India's Highest Paid Executives', *Business India,* November 7, p62.

Talmor, Eli and James S Wallace (2001): 'A Unified Analysis of Executive Pay: The Case of the Financial Sector', Working Paper – Yale School of Management's Economics Research Network.

Abramovitz, Moses (1956): 'Resources and Output Trends in United States Since 1870', *American Economic Review,* Vol. 46, No. 2, pp. 5-23.

Ahulawalia, I.J. (1985): *Industrial Growth in India: Stagnation sine the Mid-Sixties,* Oxford University Press, New Delhi.

–(1991): *Productivity and Growth in Indian Manufacturing,* Oxford University Press, Delhi.

Balakrishnan, P., K. Pushpangadan and M. Suresh Babu (2000): 'Trade Liberalization and Productivity Growth in Manufacturing: Evidence from Firm Level Panel Data', *Economic and Political Weekly,* October 7, pp. 3679-82.

Bartelsman, Eric J. and Mark Doms (2000): 'Understanding Productivity: Lessons from Longitudinal Micro Data', *Journal of Economic Literature,* Vol. 38, pp. 569-94.

Brahmananda, P.R. (1982): *Productivity in Indian Economy: Rising Inputs for Falling Outputs,* Himalaya Publishing House, Delhi.

Das, Deb Kussum (2004): "Manufacturing Productivity under Varying Trade Regimes, 1980-2000', *Economic and Political Weekly,* January 31, pp 423-33.

Feinberg, Susan and Sumit K. Majumdar (2001): 'Technology Spillover from Foreign Direct Investment in the Indian Pharmaceutical Industry', *Journal of International Business Studies,* Vol. 32, pp. 139-55.

Index